the girl's guide
to being a boss
(without being a bitch)

the girl's guide to being a boss

(without being a bitch)

VALUABLE LESSONS, SMART SUGGESTIONS,
AND TRUE STORIES FOR SUCCEEDING AS THE
CHICK-IN-CHARGE

Caitlin Friedman
and Kimberly Yorio

MORGAN ROAD BOOKS

new york

MORGAN ROAD BOOKS

Published by Morgan Road Books, an imprint of The Doubleday Broadway
Publishing Group, a division of Random House, Inc.

PRINTED IN THE UNITED STATES OF AMERICA

MORGAN ROAD BOOKS and the M colophon are trademarks of Random House, Inc.

Visit our Web site at www.morganroadbooks.com

Book design by Caroline Cunningham

Library of Congress Cataloging-in-Publication Data
Friedman, Caitlin.
    The girl's guide to being a boss (without being a bitch) : valuable lessons,
    smart suggestions, and true stories for succeeding as the chick-in-charge / by
    Caitlin Friedman and Kimberly Yorio.
        p. cm.
    Includes index.
    1. Supervision of employees—Handbooks, manuals, etc. 2. Women
    supervisors. 3. Women executives. I. Yorio, Kimberly. II. Title.

HF5549.12.F76 2006
658.3'02082—dc22

                                                    2005044759

ISBN-13: 978-0-7679-2284-5
ISBN-10: 0-7679-2284-0

10 9 8 7 6 5 4 3 2 1

To my partner in love, and life, Andrew, and my two

new joys, Declan and Taylor

To the boys who love me even on the rare occasions

when I am being a bitch, Sean and Thomas

contents

acknowledgments ix

introduction xi

one   you're a big girl now

FROM JUST ANOTHER EMPLOYEE TO CHICK-IN-CHARGE   1

two   the big picture

WHAT IT TAKES TO BECOME A GREAT LEADER   25

three   team building

YOU'RE ONLY AS GOOD AS YOUR STAFF   48

four   don't try this at work

TEN WAYS TO ALIENATE YOUR STAFF   78

five   communicate. motivate. celebrate.   98

six   delegation is not a dirty word
        EMPLOYING YOUR EMPLOYEES   117

seven playing goddess
        EVALUATIONS, PROMOTIONS, AND GIVING THE AX   136

eight culture is queen
        CORPORATE CULTURE 101   155

nine   office politics are a big fat drag
        NAVIGATING CLOSED DOORS, HUSHED WHISPERS, AND
        WATERCOOLER RUMORS   175

ten   being the boss without being bossy
        BUSINESS LESSONS YOU LEARNED IN CHILDHOOD   194

        a final note   213
        resources   215
        index   219

acknowledgments

First and foremost we want to thank the two people who were behind getting this project on the shelves, publisher Amy Hertz, who is as committed as we are to helping women be women in the workplace, and our agent, David Black, who from the morning we met with him about our books has been our champion and cheerleader. Thanks to the girls at Morgan Road Books: Anne Watters for coming up with refreshingly fun and creative marketing ideas; Jean Traina for the amazing jacket and Lauren Panepinto for those girly sticky notes (we love them). Thanks to the boys at Morgan Road Books: Marc Haeringer, one fantastic editor who really got the girl voice; Nathanael Brown, an assistant we would try to steal if we didn't like Amy so much; and one of our favorite people in publicity and in all of publishing . . . David Drake. Our foreign rights hot shot, Leigh Ann Elisco from the David Black Agency, has been a gift from the gods. We want to give a shout out to all the girls who were willing to share their stories—good, bad, and ugly—and a special thank-you to Anat Baron, Christine Deussen, and Melissa Clark, who tapped into their wide network of women to help us with this book. Thank you moms, grandmothers, sisters, aunts, friends, soon-to-be friends, and every girl out there committed to making the professional world a better place, especially Kara and Sharyn Yorio, Chrisi Colabella, and Laurice Duffy.

Caitlin wants to thank Kim for making every new business meeting, book signing, road trip, speaking engagement, and media appearance just that much more fun. And Kim wants to thank Caitlin because without her ideas and confidence the *Girl's Guides* wouldn't exist.

introduction

While writing our first book, *The Girl's Guide to Starting Your Own Business*, we had to edit the chapter "Being a Boss Sucks" down from an unreasonable two hundred pages. Why so long? Because we have both struggled with the leadership role since hiring our first assistant, and had a lot to say about its challenges, as did most of the women we interviewed. The upshot . . . managing is hard. Over the past year our little public relations agency has tripled in size, raising a bunch of questions we hadn't faced before: Who do you promote? Who do you fire? How do you effectively train an employee? How long do you invest in employees before you can expect them to pay off? How do you demonstrate gratitude for a job well done without going broke? But the biggest question that we have struggled with and continue to on almost a daily basis is: how to own and enjoy the role of boss lady.

After a lot of thought—and even more research—we've come to learn that too many women in the workforce (including us!) haven't had the chance to learn from positive female role models. Without positive experiences to draw from, we've ended up repeating bad behavior. We are hoping that this book will provide the insight and positive reinforcement so many of us have searched for in our own professional lives.

With some introspection, research, and interviews with lots of ladies who lead, we have come to the conclusion that women actually have it in them to be better managers than their male counterparts. If we could just get over our fears, the traits we are born with as women—nurturing, patience, strength, wisdom, and resourceful-ness—are the very characteristics that will make us stars in the boardroom and the mentor many employees need.

By owning the role of queen bee in a positive way, we are empow-ering you to become that one-in-a-million manager. You can be powerful without being possessive. You can be opinionated without being brassy. You can have a strong voice without micromanaging. You can be mentors who lead, inspire, and motivate.

There is no fast track to owning this role, or even getting better at it, but we think after reading *The Girl's Guide to Being a Boss (Without Being a Bitch)* you will be well on your way.

the girl's guide
to being a boss
(without being a bitch)

one

you're a big girl now

FROM JUST ANOTHER EMPLOYEE TO CHICK-IN-CHARGE

Okay. So you're the boss now. The supervisor. The manager. The captain. The taskmaster. Those days of taking orders, running errands, and clock-watching are over forever. At last, you get to call the shots.

As exciting as all this might seem, once the rush of the promotion is over, you might be scratching your head wondering exactly what your new responsibilities entail. Many feel a little lost once we arrive at the grown-up table, not having had many positive managerial role models. Fear not. You know you can do the job; all you need is a little helpful advice to send you on your way.

Whether you supervise two as a shift manager or lord over an entire corporate empire, we will help you take the leap from mediocre to marvelous. And for those of you who are already running the show, we can help you lose that nickname "Bitch on Wheels" and become the leader your employees deserve.

We'll show you what it means to be queen: how to wield your ever-evolving bag of management tricks; discover what is expected of you; decide what you can reasonably expect of your team; and how to jump in and love every minute of your Head Honchoness.

good days and bad days: the good, bad, and ugly aspects of being a manager

Leading can be a daunting task. In some ways it can be positively thrilling. In others, it can be a big old pain in the ass. Just as the freedom, responsibility, and respect start to lift you to cloud nine, the paranoia, fear, and anxiety can bring you crashing back down to earth. Like all things, being the recognized leader can have its highs and lows. Here's a look at the lawns on both sides of the fence.

the good

MONEY, MONEY, MONEY, MONEY, **MONEY**!

We might be dreaming, but if you've gotten a promotion, we'd like to assume a nice, whopping raise came along with it. Hopefully you will never again have to struggle to make ends meet and face your credit card bills at the end of the month in tears. Even if the new job doesn't mean a giant windfall, being the boss should put you in a better financial position than you were in before. And if you're not, make sure you check out the sections in chapter 5 on fair pay and lobby for what you deserve.

PRINCESS OF POWER

Power is good. Making decisions that lead to positive outcomes is good. Making the calls, changing the rules, and forging decisions that may alter the course of the entire company can be great. Having the ultimate responsibility is positively thrilling. The bitch boss who throws her weight around, barks orders, and is generally focused on herself while making her employees miserable doesn't have to be you. Once you settle into your new role, you'll find that being the leader means you can be the manager who uplifts employees and gets real enjoyment from watching your colleagues grow and prosper. Building a team, working together, and teaching others will be hugely gratifying. At the end of the day, it can make you feel like a million bucks.

THE MORE YOU KNOW
While mentoring your dewy protégées, you yourself will be acquiring new information and facing fresh and exciting challenges every day. Learned knowledge changes us and makes us better mothers, friends, and businesswomen. Growing professionally can be empowering and give you a broader perspective on both the world and your place within it. The more you know the better off you are, both intellectually and résuméwise. Don't forget the journey to becoming a great leader is a lifelong one.

YOUR MOM WILL BE PROUD
Ultimately, if you succeed, the prestige and glow of success will make all the mistakes and missteps worthwhile. There is no greater feeling in the world than a job well done.

the bad

TRAINING ANYONE?
The sad reality is there's never enough training offered to employees. Even among the companies that have well-established training

programs, there will be plenty of times when you just don't know what to do. You would think that when a new person is hired they would be handed all the necessary tools to do a job effectively. Maybe the person before you fled the job or was fired, and the people who remain don't really know what she did. Perhaps everyone is too busy to sit down and go through your job in detail. Whatever the reason, your training will probably consist of "Here's your office. Good luck." It's up to you to figure out how to achieve your goals using the best resource you have—your staff.

IT'S LONELY AT THE TOP

For all of the positive things your new role as a manager can bring, the scariest one is the isolation you will feel as the woman at the top of the corporate ladder. You have the responsibility to make your team a success, and if it fails, you take the blame. Gone are the days when you can be everyone's gal pal. No more shuffling off to the lunchroom to spend an hour shooting the breeze about the latest episode of *Desperate Housewives*. When asked the biggest mistake that new managers make, 90 percent of the women whom we interviewed replied that they tried to be liked. You are not there to be anyone's friend. You are in the leadership role to provide the tools and environment that your team needs to accomplish their goals. If the team is not accomplishing the goals, with all the appropriate support, then you, new manager, will have to reprimand and maybe terminate team members who aren't measuring up. This power that you gain when promoted will separate you from your team.

KEEP THE PERSONAL, PERSONAL AND NEVER LET THEM SEE YOU SWEAT

This is a tough one. No matter how bad it gets, no matter what kind of a day you're having, you absolutely, positively cannot freak out. It doesn't matter if your car died in the middle of the interstate on the way to work, or that you just found out your husband has been having an affair. Your personal problems should not come into the workplace. At Ann's first job as an assistant, her boss was trying to adopt a baby. She had a special cell phone just for potential birth mothers to call. When her boss was in a meeting, Ann was required to man the baby phone. If a potential birth mother called, Ann would have to chase down her boss. If her boss couldn't be disturbed, she would have to interview the potential birth mother and try to schedule a time for a callback. Ann was honored at the amount of trust put in her by her boss, but scared to death that if she messed up the baby phone, not only was she jeopardizing her job, she could potentially cause her boss to lose the baby she was so desperately trying to get. While adopting a baby was obviously the priority for her boss, it was unfair to make it Ann's responsibility.

THE BUCK STOPS WITH YOU

The team's problems are now your problems—individually and collectively. As a matter of fact, everyone's problems become your problems. If a member of your group has a sick child and can't be there for the ten o'clock meeting with the biggest client, then you have to figure out a way to cover for her without the client ever knowing. If your top account executive loses the biggest account, and your department won't make its numbers, then *you* will have to find a replacement account or shrink the team to cover the shortfall. And at the very least, you will have to take the heat from your management. If someone on your team opens an e-mail from her boyfriend that infects your entire office with a virus, erasing all your records from the last five years, then you and the IT department have a very big problem. No more hiding until the storm blows over. It will be your responsibility to mobilize the team, board up the windows, and evacuate.

DISCIPLINE, WRITE-UPS, AND THE PINK SLIP

Delivering bad news is never easy; deciding to severely impact someone's livelihood by terminating them because they can't cut the mustard, just plain sucks. We've devoted almost an entire upcoming chapter to the *f*-word, firing.

the ugly

NOWHERE TO GO BUT DOWN

With each step you climb up the corporate ladder, the farther down you will go if you fall off. You will exist in constant fear of living up to expectations (although the rest of the group shouldn't know it), getting the job done effectively, and accomplishing the team's goals. The higher you go, the more you're under scrutiny from the ones beneath you who think they can do your job better and the ones above you who think they are paying you too much. If you don't create positive relationships from the get-go, those go-getters will take every opportunity to prove that they are more suited to your job. We're not suggesting you become paranoid, but suggest that you remain aware of the changing dynamics of your senior position. In an upcoming chapter, we will explore why management experts recommend forging relationships with those above, below and equal to you in the organization.

THE RAP SHEET: CELLULOID BITCH BOSSES

KILL BILL (2003)—Lucy Liu as O-Ren Ishii, the Evil Crime Boss of Tokyo's Underworld. When one of her peers questions her leadership, she cuts his head off without missing a beat.

Lesson: You need to have an open door policy for all your employees so they can speak their minds. Firing or reprimanding someone just for disagreeing with you is unacceptable.

DISCLOSURE (1994)—Demi Moore as Meredith Johnson. She comes on to her employee, then acts like he sexually harassed her. Evil ensues through lies and cover-ups.

Lesson: Never, ever, ever, ever hit on or flirt with an employee, and never use sex to leverage your power. Granted, Demi's problems in this movie go deeper than that, but your own sexuality should never come into play in the workplace.

WORKING GIRL (1988)—Sigourney Weaver as Katharine Parker. Steals her employee's idea, then gets it in the end when her employee steals her life.

Lesson: Never take credit for a coworker's or subordinate's hard work. You'll look like a bitch and lose the trust of your employees. Not to mention you might find yourself as the target of a good case of revenge.

TRUTH OR DARE (1991)—Madonna as herself. In this documentary of the material girl, she is revealed as the worst kind of boss. She exerts a sort of maternal control over her dancers, going from being their best friend to being a total bitch.

Lesson: Bipolar Betty has no place in the office. You have to remain consistent, loyal, and unbiased with all your employees no matter how badly they screw up.

RAISING HELEN (2004)—Helen Mirren as Dominique. As the boss of a modeling agency, when her employee inherits her sister's kids, she proves the workplace is less than family-friendly by stealing her clients and belittling her in front of the staff for being late to a meeting.

Lesson: Yes, you have to think of the company's well-being first, but in the end it is the staff that is the company. As long as the work is getting done, you can create a positive and flexible work environment for your team.

101 DALMATIANS (1996)—Glenn Close as Disney über-villainess Cruella De Vil. Not only is she a puppy killer, in this live-action version of the classic cartoon she terrorizes her employees at her fashion design firm by screaming, throwing things, and generally humiliating all of those who work for her.

Lesson: Never lead with fear. It is possible to have a firm hand and still enjoy the respect of your colleagues. Using terror tactics is never the way to make your office function efficiently. Firm but fair is the way to go.

CATWOMAN (2004)—Sharon Stone as Laurel Hedare. When her employee figures out that the "miracle" anti-aging face cream her cosmetics company makes has terrible side effects, Laurel actually resorts to murder to prevent her from revealing the truth.

Lesson: A. Never lie to your employees. B. If you do, be ready to face the repercussions when the truth is revealed.

the job: key functions and roles

Though the responsibilities of any management job can vary wildly depending on what business you're in, there are a few elemental duties you'll be asked to perform that translate across the board. We'll touch on these here first, but go into each in greater detail in the upcoming chapters.

YOU WILL HIRE, FIRE, EVALUATE, AND PROMOTE

Putting together your team and keeping it in line will be your most important role as a manager. You will need to decide if additional employees are needed and can be afforded. You must provide constant access to and evaluate the ones you have. If the creative department is swamped, staying late every night, and bickering because they are burned out, it is up to you to decide how to help ease the workload.

In our research, the single biggest criticism we heard about women managers is that they are too emotional. They should just be more professional. After all, business is just business. But is it? Business is actually done through the coming together of a number of individuals with very different styles and personalities. And as a manager, you will have to find a way to make them the most productive they can be.

Hiring, firing, evaluating, and promoting are the most emotional decisions you can make. Take hiring, for example. A responsible hiring manager will solicit a number of résumés, weed them down to the top candidates, interview the candidates a few times, check references, and then make a decision. When faced with a few candidates with similar strengths, how do you choose? You try and figure out who will be the best personality fit for the group and hope for the best.

When it doesn't work out, then you have to fire. And don't tell us that firing employees isn't an emotional exercise. You are taking away a person's livelihood and perhaps that of their family too. Emotions come into play. The trick for women is to be able to manage their emotions as well as they manage staff. Consistency is the best you can hope for and is probably good enough to keep the emotional criticism out of the office.

YOU WILL HAVE A PLAN AND DELEGATE WORK TO YOUR EMPLOYEES

For those times your staff isn't in flux, creating a business plan and delegating its various aspects will be your main managerial task. This includes earmarking what needs to be accomplished on a daily, weekly, monthly, yearly, and long-term basis, making a schedule and determining who on your team is best to handle each assignment. You will be asking questions such as: Is this a one-woman job? Would putting your workers into teams be more productive?

Delegating doesn't just mean telling your team what to do. You have to make sure they understand the project and how best to achieve its goal. Communication is the only way to make sure everyone stays on schedule. Checking in on a regular basis through progress reports and being involved will ensure the job gets done right.

Every manager has to delegate, but according to www.advancing women.com, many women are reluctant to delegate. They cite a number of reasons, including:

- Most of us succeed because we are good at mastering certain types of details.
- It's human nature to like to do what we're good at doing.
- Successful women are often perfectionists.
- If we do it ourselves, we know it will be perfect, or, at least, as perfect as we can make it.

YOU WILL PROVIDE GUIDANCE, DIRECTION, MOTIVATION, AND INSPIRATION TO YOUR EMPLOYEES

When a longtime employee comes to you with questions on how a new system works, you will be the woman who listens intently to the problem and ultimately provides the answers. Say one of your salespeople feels like the company's current marketing techniques aren't quite bringing the customers in. She arrives at your office door with a load of new ideas. At this point, your direction is imperative, and together you can sort it out and make the right decision.

Or let's imagine profits are down, the competition is taking you to the cleaners, and morale in the office is at an all-time low. This is your opportunity to lead, to motivate, to inspire, and make your staff believe in the product/company/mission with a passion they've never felt before. Call in a research firm to help distinguish what edge your competitor has and then lead a brainstorming session to develop ways to combat it. Organize a group retreat where everyone can come together and hash out their issues and problems, then work together to find a solution. Providing guidance and inspiration to your staff will be the most challenging part of your job, but ultimately the most fulfilling.

YOU WILL SUPERVISE AND MAINTAIN THE FISCAL HEALTH OF THE COMPANY AND/OR DEPARTMENT

Whether you are given a budget to follow or have to create guidelines from scratch, it will be your responsibility to stay within the parameters of the planned spending. If your department has a quarterly budget of $200,000, your job is to allocate resources so that you come in under or on that planned spending limit. Be prepared to explain why if you don't.

Managing budgets can include finding ways to cut back on staff if your payroll is ballooning, or shifting monies from one project to another if one needs additional funding. It will also mean finding new ways to boost your profit margin so that your bottom line is expanded. If you never had to handle money before, you will be working it like a casino dealer before you know it.

YOU WILL BE EXPECTED TO ANSWER FOR YOUR STAFF, DEPARTMENT, OR BRANCH

No matter what level of leader you are, you will still have to answer to someone. As an entrepreneur, ultimately your customers will have the last say if the quality of your product starts to falter. In most managerial jobs there is someone above you calling the shots, whether you are a district manager, branch supervisor, or the head of your department. You will be expected to answer up the chain of management. You have to be confident when dealing with senior management and defend your department or to take the responsibility for missteps. Just as you need to communicate with your employees, you must keep an open line between you and your boss.

YOU WILL ACT AS A BUFFER BETWEEN YOUR EMPLOYEES AND ANY MANAGEMENT ABOVE YOU

Your top store manager screwed up the product returns, leaving your region $50,000 in the hole. When the boss finds out and comes down on you tenfold, you have to take the brunt of the hit, yet pass it down in a way that is productive and supportive to your employees. No matter how badly the chairman of the board might behave toward you, you can't pass that negative reinforcement down. You are responsible for the actions of your staff. Hopefully, in delegation and direction, you've made the right decisions, so whatever goes wrong, you are largely to blame. Any antagonistic energy you get from above has to be recycled into positive change.

good witch or big bitch?

MINIMUM TASKS, MAXIMUM HUMILIATION

When Jenny was looking for a career change, she was thrilled to read that a local public relations company was in need of a publicity assistant. Even better, the owner of the agency was reputed to be one of the best in the business, a real dynamo and a great person to learn from. The interview was a breeze and Jenny was promised lots of opportunities, including working with the media. The trade-off, her future boss would tell her, was that "you will have to run the office, which shouldn't take more than a few hours a week." By the end of her first week, it was clear that what she would actually be doing is running the office while squeezing in a few media calls on her lunch breaks.

Jenny could handle the bait and switch. What she couldn't handle was the treatment she received from the owner of the business. On top of the choice assignments—cleaning the storeroom, ordering pens and other office supplies, returning her boss's rented videos to a local mall, packing and shipping hundreds of items every week. Three or four times a day the owner of the business would hop on the office-wide intercom to demand that Jenny run up to her office to clean out her outbox. Every time Jenny heard the three beeps indicating a page, her stomach would drop because she knew that it meant passing her colleagues—busy talking on their phones—on her way to pick up a pile of personal notes and to-do lists waiting for her in the outbox.

Jenny's downfall? She was too good at her job. A model of efficiency, she got the office running like clockwork. She updated the files and negotiated phone rates and everyone was happy. Except Jenny. As the weeks went by, her colleagues, picking up on the demeaning manner in which she was treated by the owner, began taking advantage of her too. Her contribution to Monday morning meetings was soon taking supply orders from the rest of the staff. The media call assignments became increasingly infrequent as her day became filled with padded envelopes and paper clips. When she confronted the owner of the business, she replied, "Give it time, now here's my outbox."

Jenny lasted eight months at the job, wanting to have something to add to her résumé, but hating every day of it. More than that, she hated her boss.

Big Bitch. Your most important job as a manager is to inspire and keep good employees. Jenny was a superstar. She handled her assignments with efficiency and good cheer. The staff liked and respected her until they watched her manager belittle her accomplishments and devalue her contribution by interrupting her to sort her mail. Jenny could have been a key member of the team for years to come; instead, she quit as soon as she could find another boss.

From *The American Heritage Dictionary*, fourth edition:

> Management: 1. The act, manner, or practice of managing; handling, supervision, or control. 2. The person or persons who control or direct a business or other enterprise.
>
> Manager: 1. One who handles, controls, or directs.

Even the dictionary tells you. Managing is about control. But controlling people is never as easy as it should be. Women be wary.

movin' on up: new expectations

Now that you're in a management role, you will no longer have someone looking over your shoulder and telling you what to do every minute of the day. No one is responsible for you now except you. Owning up to your job responsibilities will be the key to your ultimate success.

Here are fifteen things you should always do now that you are responsible for yourself and your team.

1. Create a to-do list

Since no one will be delegating to you, it is up to you to keep an eye on what needs to be done. Creating a to-do list is one of the best ways to prioritize and keep track. With a list to reference, small things will never fall through the cracks and you'll always have the next step at your fingertips.

2. Set goals

What do you want to accomplish in your new position? More than anyone, you know what you are capable of, and it is up to you to set goals not just for yourself but for the company as a whole. Set goals and stick with them. Daily, monthly, even long-term planning can mean the difference between what does and doesn't get done.

3. Stick to deadlines

A deadline is a deadline. A promise to a client to have a commercial developed, cast, and filmed by a certain date should be set in stone. A date ultimatum from the head office for the grand opening of the new store should be treated as gospel. A pledge to your staff to complete evaluations before the Christmas holidays should be met even if it means working late over Thanksgiving to get it done. If you can't hold strong to a set deadline, how can you expect your employees to do the same?

4. Keep your word

A new employee is promised a raise in six months during contract negotiations. A customer is offered a full refund if the face cream she ordered doesn't make her look ten years younger. A peer asks if you'll take her report home over the weekend and get it back to her before she has to show it to your boss on Monday. When you say you are going to do something, make sure you do it. Nothing is worth more in business than trust.

5. Get it in writing

Now that you are responsible for others, make sure that everyone is clear about their objectives. The easiest way to get everyone on the same page is to put it all down on paper.

6. Be proactive about everything you do

Don't wait for directions and a map. Get to work. If your team is assigned a project that is new, sit down together and figure out how to get it done. If a new advertising plan for your company seems to be backfiring, figure out how to fix it. Don't sit idly by.

7. Treat your aspect of the business like an entrepreneur

Understanding what everyone in your department does will ensure that you always know what is going on. Let's say shoplifting in your stores is on the rise; work with the security team to come up with ways to prevent it. Don't think about your business unit or responsibilities individually, but of how you can contribute to the bigger picture.

8. Contribute to the team

Not only must you pull your own weight, but you must prove to the staff that you're not afraid to get your hands dirty. Acting as part of the troupe will not only help you run your business more effectively, but it will also win you the respect of those above you, below you, and across from you.

9. Think big picture

Up until this point in your career, you've been asked to take on one task and work closely on the details. As you move up the corporate ladder, you'll become more focused on the big picture while the team supporting you should be obsessing over the details.

10. Be your own cheerleader

Being the boss can be a thankless job. No one is going to hold your hand and tell you what a great job you're doing anymore. You have to depend on yourself for all those high fives. When you've worked hard and accomplished a goal, take yourself out to lunch, get a massage, or arrange for a day out of the office.

11. Sell your accomplishments to those above you

No one is going to be there to witness it when you do something amazing. Don't be afraid to toot your own horn to your higher-ups. If you are uncomfortable selling yourself, use the opportunity to pump up the team. Not only will this make your team look hot, it will endear you to your boss as a great leader. Hey, if you don't work it for yourself, who will?

12. Stick up for yourself

Hopefully, in the past, you had someone looking out for you when things got rough or someone tried to pass an undeserved buck in your direction. More than likely, you won't have that person now. If you feel like you are being unfairly treated, don't feel too intimidated to take a stand. Again, if you don't, who will?

13. Don't take things personally

Geraldine Ferraro might still have a vibrant political career if she hadn't taken some partisan bashing to heart and wept in front of the nation. You have to have thick skin in the business world and realize that just because someone gets mad, you get passed over for a raise, or your management hands off a project to another district manager, it doesn't mean you stink. Handle disappointments with class. Remember, this advice swings both ways for those days you have to discipline a friend or take a hard worker off an account because he hasn't pulled his weight.

14. Don't forget to network

Alliance-building is what gets people to the winner's circle on reality game shows, and it is what you will need to do in order to make it in the rough-and-tumble world of business. Meet as many people in and out of your field as you can. Spend your time building positive perceptions and do anything you can to help others out. The more people who respect you as a professional, the better off you'll be when you need to call in a favor. Not only will these folks be able to help you out at one point or another, but they'll also be a valuable support group and sometimes even become lifelong friends.

15. Find a mentor

Seek out someone within your company or within your same field who has more experience than you. Someone you can learn from. Someone who might be willing to take you under her wing and impart all her worldly wisdom. Making this kind of connection early on can help you through the best and worst of times. Nothing beats having someone you can go to for managerial advice and support.

the word

LINDA BRIERTY, THERAPIST

Why do you think that women are so afraid of being perceived as a bitch in the workplace?

Without perpetuating gender stereotypes, let me address this. Some women may fear their own power and leadership, and this power is not always encouraged, or even allowed in certain settings. Strong women may be viewed as intimidating. There may be actual negative consequences for speaking up.

Many women have been conditioned to want acceptance and approval from others, at times to our own self-detriment. This relates to the historical role of caretaking others and neglecting ourselves. Self-advocacy and self-care, all those "self" words in fact, may have been perceived as "selfish."

It is commonly known that when a woman behaves like her male counterparts in the workplace, she is often negatively labeled. If she is assertive or stands her ground, she is called tough. If she is matter-of-fact and not emotional, she is cold. The expectations are skewed by gender, despite the progress that has been made. This can discourage assertive behavior, and effectively keep women down even in the present day. Because we may respond to the world emotionally as well as intellectually, it may be hard to separate our feelings from the work itself. We may fear rejection or have dependency issues, including the need to be liked and part of the group. This may supercede owning our own power.

For those first-time managers, do you have any advice about how they can begin to overcome their fears about telling others what to do?

First-time managers can remind themselves that this is not high school. This is not a popularity contest, although a firm grasp of people skills is extremely important. If you alienate your staff, your productivity will suffer. If everyone is motivated, it will soar. Remember, employees are people with feelings. Using constructive feedback instead of personal criticism is important. Leaving everyone's self-esteem intact is crucial.

When you are delegating or instructing someone, it is about the facts. You are simply trying to get a job done. It is not personal, and it is wise to move the emotions out of the way, and keep most discussions matter-of-fact and productive. If there is a problem, it is identified not as a character assassination, but as an issue to be resolved. You can then develop solutions to leave the conversation on a high note. It is also important to identify employees' strengths. You should anticipate a degree of anger and resentment from employees, simply by virtue of the authority figure role you find yourself in. It goes with the territory. Be flattered. Remember, you will also be a lightning rod for employees "transferential reactions," meaning feelings from previous relationships with authority figures will be projected onto you. Don't take it personally, don't respond personally.

Owning your power means leading others in a respectful way. You will not always be liked; however, you will need to be respected to maintain your authority in the position. You will need to establish and maintain professional boundaries with people. Be prepared: It can be lonely. You will not be able to be part of the peer group. You will be talked about.

Do you have any confidence boosters for women—things they can think about or do to feel good about themselves?

You have to summon up confidence in yourself because of all your wonderful qualities. You have to maintain a supportive inner dialogue. Turn off the "inner critic" and practice self-love. If you don't have that, the world can knock you over more easily. If you act and speak on your own behalf, you are taking care of yourself. Remember, we are trained to caretake others, so this is a conscious reversal. We are no longer the exception to our own care and attention. There is nothing wrong with liking yourself, encouraging yourself—this is not a deadly sin of pride. Our light shines brighter this way, and we can refuse to turn down our flame for anyone. When you get beyond your own ego, you can actually do more in and for the world.

no free time?: balancing home, family, and friends

It's easy to get caught up in the thrill of doing a good job; working our fingers to the bone, putting in late hours, and driving into the office on the weekends. We once had a boss who kept handwritten crayon signs by her desk that read, "Remember, Mom, family comes first." We never wanted to be that kind of friend or mother, and we've made a conscious effort to find the right balance between our private and work lives. Here are a few thoughts on how to have a social and home life and still get the job done.

ORGANIZING YOUR TIME AT HOME

The better you organize your time at home, the more time you will have to spend with your family and friends. Make lists and keep schedules so that home duties can run just as efficiently as the ones you have at work. Some great calendar programs are available online that allow you to input the entire family's schedules, including the nanny, and it will automatically send reminders for car pools and doctor's appointments. This is especially helpful with divorced parents, as it offers a neutral place for all parties to keep track of the schedule. We recommend www.ourfamilywizard.com.

DON'T FORGET YOUR FRIENDS

Friendships can often be just as important as family life. It's a total release to get together with your girlfriends and pretend you're sixteen again. If you find it difficult to catch up with them, plan a monthly girls' night, and make a pact to always be there, no matter what. We have a monthly book group that has been meeting for years, and as we have all gone up the ladder at our jobs, the conversations have moved from complaining about our bosses to the challenges of being a boss. Kim goes to girls' weekend twice a year with her high school friends and will often extend a business trip with a Saturday night stay if she is in a city where she has a friend. Your employer won't mind because the reduced cost of the airfare generally more than covers the cost of an extra night in the hotel.

STAY UPBEAT

No matter how hairy things get at work or how crazy life can be at home, try to keep a positive outlook. Nothing wastes time and zaps energy more than a bad attitude. Believe us, it's not always easy. When we're really down and frustrated with work, we focus our energy on turning one negative into a positive. We like results. For example, if we're feeling the pressure of no cash flow in the business, we devote twenty minutes each to collections, calling and e-mailing clients pressuring them to pay our overdue bills. This little exercise cheers us up in a number of ways: 1) We get the benefit about feeling good about solving a problem; 2) we immediately see the light at the end of the tunnel because we know when monies are coming in; and 3) it reinvigorates our energy to do good work and get new business because we love getting paid.

If we're feeling pressured that we're not generating enough media for a client, we'll stop everything and each of us will spend twenty minutes pitching new media outlets. Invariably we secure a placement, and again we are cheered up at making a positive change in our situation.

TIME FOR YOU
Most important of all, you have to carve out time for yourself; otherwise you will never be able to juggle everything and still maintain your sanity. Wake up a half hour earlier than the rest of your family to enjoy that first cup of coffee in peace. Steal away to a yoga class for a midday detox.

girl talk

STACY MADISON, COFOUNDER, STACY'S PITA CHIP COMPANY

After a four-year career in social work, Stacy met Stacy's Pita Chip Company cofounder Mark Andrus. Stacy and Mark quickly discovered that they were both lifelong "foodies," and each longed for a career in the food industry. After deciding to go into business together, Stacy and Mark moved back to the East Coast, where Stacy's Pita Chip Company was born. As founder of a leading woman-owned business, Stacy was invited to the White House in 1999. Additionally, she was honored in 2004 by Jewish Women International as one of the U.S. and Israel's Top Ten Women to Watch. The company also received the prestigious 2004 Greater Boston Chamber of Commerce Small Business of the Year award and was honored with the Fleet Bank Entrepreneur of the Year award.

What was your first management experience?
I guess I was a born leader. My third-grade teacher used to say I was "too much of a social butterfly," but being friendly really helped when it came to motivating and managing people. My first job was

as the assistant manager of a surf-themed restaurant and I managed about thirty employees. It's not that I was friends with my staff, although I liked them personally. I think people felt comfortable talking problems over with me, rather than building conflict or resentments. Even before I was a trained social worker, I was a big believer in talking through things, so I faced issues head-on.

What did you learn about yourself when you first began to manage a staff?

I learned how difficult it was to maintain balance between different types of personalities and that I had to constantly be aware of staying objective, not emotional.

Can you share with us your first firing experience?

At my first restaurant job, I had to fire a waiter. I felt so bad about it that it ended up being more like a therapy session than a termination. At the time, I had never been fired myself, and I felt soooo bad, I could only imagine what this poor kid was feeling. I talked to the waiter for over an hour, reassuring him of his value and worth, even though we were firing him. It was rough. I think I felt more traumatized than he did!

What is your favorite thing about managing people?

I love to give people a chance to work independently and to experience the joy that comes from the autonomy and being proud of their own work.

How have you applied what you learned as a manager to your home life?

I have learned the value of instilling independence and self-confidence. By seeing how employees have flourished when they were given a lot of responsibility, I can see myself as the kind of parent who gives their kids a lot of independence and responsibility.

What do you look for when you hire someone?

So much depends on personality. Being a part of a privately held company, when each person is hired they are becoming part of a team or family. Almost every job out there can be learned, but working together with others is not something that can be taught. I would have to say that finding a good personality fit is 98 percent of the ball game.

How do you motivate employees?

It's always nice to motivate people financially, but that's not always possible. Find out what makes people tick and there are lots of little ways to reward them. It's also extremely important to recognize contributions and not take advantage of the fact that people are working hard for you. Someone can have a terrific job where they make lots of money, but hate going to work every day. If you create an atmosphere where people love their job, it could be life changing.

Do you have advice for first-time managers?

Listen and be creative. The most important thing you can find out is what makes a person tick, in every way from benefits and vacation time to recognition, family, and favorite hobbies. That way you will know how to reward a person, other than financially.

the big picture

WHAT IT TAKES TO BECOME A GREAT LEADER

It's not easy for women to become great leaders. Forces actually conspire against them. Since the early 1980s, studies have shown that what works for men doesn't work for women in a leadership context. Those same studies also show that women are not socialized to become leaders and that great leading female role models are few and far between. Sure, there's Eleanor Roosevelt, Hillary Clinton, Madeleine Albright, Oprah Winfrey, and Maya Angelou, but beyond that, can you name anyone? When searching for Internet sites, the only one that comes up devoted to women leaders throughout history is a personal site called www.guide2womenleaders.com, and it's written and maintained by a Danish *man*!

Whether you've just been promoted or are planning for the future, now is the time to make sure you have the right stuff to be a great boss, not just a good one. But where do you begin?

This is not an easy or quick process. For most, it will take a lifetime of work to become an admired and valuable leader. You must adopt effective strategies and habits now that will set you on the right path. What's most important, though, is to monitor your progress and continue to learn and grow.

why being the boss doesn't always suck: what's in it for you

Think about how great you feel when you accomplish something, when you get that rush for a job well done. Crossing things off the to-do list has to be one of the most satisfying things in anyone's day. Now, multiply that feeling by five, or ten, or maybe even one hundred—that's the big payoff for bosses and leaders. Your sole job as leader or manager is to facilitate others' accomplishments. Leaders give the direction, support, inspiration, and space for the subordinate to accomplish her goals.

We are led to believe leading is the most natural skill in the world, but we're here to tell you that not only is leading not natural for most, it's damn difficult for everyone. Neither one of us is a shrinking violet, yet we find it challenging to assert our authority without feeling like the world's biggest bitches.

Leadership implies a relationship. Someone leads and someone follows. And as women know better than anyone, relationships are complicated. The other side rarely reacts as you think they will, and you need to constantly learn from your mistakes. Here's a good example.

good witch or big bitch?

FIRM, BUT FAIR

We hired a new assistant in our office. We went through a rigorous interviewing process and found an incredibly energetic, smart, and enthusiastic young woman. We explained her initial responsibilities and set her off to work. We agreed that we would spend time with her a little bit individually each day, and copy her on much of our e-mail correspondence, but we found ourselves on some crazy deadlines so we told her she would need to learn as much as possible by listening and asking questions. We didn't have much time for teaching—which is not good management. After all, we were incredibly busy with the "important" work, pitching new business, running the office, and servicing the existing clients. Our assistant was there to make our lives easier and not vice versa. We were unknowingly furthering a model we suffered under in the early part of our own careers. We were scared to death at our first jobs because our bosses had thrown us into the deep end of the pool. The sink-or-swim style of management stinks. Even the most resourceful employee will become frustrated and make mistakes.

Ten days into her tenure, a series of unfortunate events occurred. Kim was in Paris for a long Memorial Day vacation and Caitlin was holding down the fort. The Internet inexplicably went down, which obviously can be disastrous to any small business. When Kim returned from vacation, the Internet had still not been repaired and no fix date was scheduled. Kim had to take an author around to meet with editors for three days, so she wouldn't be in the office. During this time (we're now up to day thirteen of the assistant's tenure) we needed a photocopy of the author's manuscript to bring to one of our appointments. The assistant quickly prepared a copy and handed it off to Kim, who was running out the door. At the meeting with the editor of *Organic Style*, Kim and the author realized the pages of the manuscript were out of order and upside down, and that a chapter on organics was even missing.

This was humiliating. Kim knew the author expected the mistake to be addressed immediately.

In our partnership we lean on each other for certain skills that we do not possess. Kim leans on Caitlin to have the tough conversations. She has a brilliant way of remaining calm and measured in the face of conflict. Kim tends to get emotional and overreact. Kim called Caitlin and couldn't reach her. But the author was standing there expecting a resolution. Kim called the assistant and asked her to rush by messenger a clean copy of the manuscript to the editor because she had just left the editor's office and had given her an incomplete version. When she began profusely apologizing, Kim very succinctly told her there was "no reason to apologize, just please don't make that mistake again because a) it's embarrassing and b) it's unacceptable quality at our firm." After the call, the author congratulated Kim for being firm but fair.

The following evening our assistant stopped by Kim's desk, asked to schedule an appointment to speak with her, and promptly burst into tears.

"What's wrong?" Kim asked. She thought she must have had a horrible personal problem, when in fact *we* had a horrible *personnel* problem. The assistant went on to explain that she wanted to do a good job and be successful, but she needed more. She needed positive reinforcement and support—much more support. Kim wasn't to tell her what she did wrong, but what she did right. She couldn't function if Kim continued to be so negative. Kim needed to applaud her efforts and gently point out where things could be done better. Kim was shocked. Not only had she completely misread the situation, she had been applauding her own management skills.

We've told this story countless times to other managers and the feedback falls firmly into two camps: 1) Get rid of her: She's too needy and her job as the team assistant is to worry about the team and not herself, and 2) Good for her: She told you what kind of management style she needs.

It was a management lesson for us. After a few days of venting and soul-searching we realized that we had a good employee and should do everything we could to try to train her and keep her. If

someone is smart and a hard worker, then they are worth any extra effort management needs to expend to help them do their jobs
more effectively.

situational leadership: taking charge

All of the women we interviewed had their own unique philosophies
and approach to leadership. The model that works well for many
women, including us, is an approach called situational leadership.
Situational leadership is being the right girl in the right place at the
right time. Most women do this every day: They try not to get angry
with a nervous colleague on their first day, they keep close eye on
some staff because they need more supervision, or give lots of lati-
tude to those who can handle the freedom.

Our favorite management guru, Ken Blanchard, author of the
One Minute Manager series, created a model for situational leadership in *Leadership and the One Minute Manager* that allows you to analyze the needs of your employees and adopt the most appropriate
leadership style. It sounds complicated, but it's easy and makes perfect sense to us.

First, learn the four styles of Blanchard's leadership: Directing,
Coaching, Supporting, and Delegating. When you're "Directing,"
you provide very specific direction and closely monitor progress toward the goal. When you're "Coaching," you continue to direct and
closely monitor, but you also begin to explain decisions, solicit suggestions, and support progress. When you "Support," you facilitate
and support the efforts toward accomplishing tasks as well as give
employees responsibility for making their own decisions. Finally,
when you're "Delegating," you turn over responsibility for decision-
making and problem-solving to the individual.

Blanchard identifies four types of employees. He has given a little alphanumeric code for each one, which we find a bit boring and difficult to remember, so we've renamed them. Blanchard calls his "low competence, high commitment" employees D1s. We call them "young and eagers," and we wish we found more. The young and eagers are brand new to the workforce and know very little about the real world yet possess an enormous amount of enthusiasm and desire to do a good job. Blanchard's D2s are "low competence, low commitment," and we call these "get rid of 'ems." Life's too short to have people on the team who neither know what they're doing nor want to succeed. Blanchard's D3s exhibit "moderate to high competence and variable commitment." We call this group the "competent but needies"; they know what they're doing and do it well, yet need regular encouragement and support. Finally, the D4s exhibit "high competence and high commitment," and they're our "superstars."

Now put it all together. "Direct" the "young and eagers." Tell them in very clear terms what to do, how to do it, and when it needs to be done. Give the "young and eagers" systems—remember many of them have never worked before. Show them how to organize their desk, organize their work, and organize their time. Give them frequent reminders and systems for checking in—a daily to-do list in the morning and an afternoon "what got done" e-mail are great ways to keep them focused and working. We ask our assistant to do the agenda for our weekly staff meeting and then distribute the minutes. This task helps her learn our business, know what everyone is working on, and take ownership of keeping track of the team—three key pieces to her development.

If you find yourself with some "get rid of 'ems" on your team, and you have the energy to give them a chance, then "coach." Give direction and feedback and support and praise to build their self-esteem, and then involve them in decision-making to restore their commitment. Coaching can be difficult, and at the very least time-consuming. You're not just teaching an employee the responsibilities of his job, but trying to reinspire him, too. If you are going to take this on, the first step should be the "come to Jesus" meeting. Sit down with your employee and explain where things are going wrong; be specific and direct. One of our most senior and trusted employees went through a bad time. She started coming in late every day, missing deadlines and meetings, and began acting inappropriately around other members of our team. We sat her down and laid down the law—while we cared about her and respected the work she had done for us in the past, her current performance was unacceptable and it had to change immediately or she would have to find another job. We're happy to report that she completely turned it around and has been a star ever since.

"Support" your "competent but needies." They don't need you to tell them how to do their work; they just need encouragement and recognition for a job well done. Laurice Duffy, president of LDK Cleaning Service, has been running a cleaning business for ten years. In an industry where turnover is extremely high, she has had some of her crew since the day she started. The key to her success is communication. All of her employees can clean well, and she wants them to know how important their work is to the operation. After all, they are the heart of the business and she treats them as such. She spends almost 50 percent of her time communicating with her crew (not always easy because, for most, English is not their first language). She has a morning meeting when they come and pick up their supplies for the day. She reviews their schedule and points out any special instructions for specific clients. She checks in with them during the day and her supervisors call her at the end of each shift, reviewing the day's jobs. Her "girls," as she calls them, are all competent cleaners; however, they need to know that Laurice is paying attention to their work and that she appreciates all of their efforts.

If you're fortunate enough to find any "superstars" on your team, then "delegate" responsibilities and projects to them. They know what to do and how to do it and don't relish you looking over their shoulders. They should be recognized for their accomplishments and promoted through the ranks. The "superstars" are rare and won't stay around unless you make their career development your priority. Engage them in their work process. Do they want a weekly update meeting with you? A daily e-mail? A monthly check-in? A combination of the above? Let them set the schedule and come to you when they need to. Remember that your best people will work through these stages of development, and that if you give someone new responsibilities, they may be working at a different level in those areas while continuing to excel in the parts of their job where they have more experience.

the word

LIBBY SARTAIN, CHIEF PEOPLE, YAHOO!

Libby Sartain is senior vice president, Human Resources and Chief People, Yahoo! With more than twenty-five years of experience in human resource management, Libby is responsible for leading Yahoo! Inc.'s global human resources efforts and managing and developing the human resources team. She also focuses on attracting, retaining, and developing employees who will promote and strengthen the company culture, as well as represent the powerful Yahoo! brand.

Prior to joining Yahoo! in August 2001, Sartain was "vice president of people" at Southwest Airlines. An employee of Southwest Airlines since 1988, Sartain managed a staff of three hundred and led all human resources functions at the airline, including employment, training, benefits, and compensation. She also played a key role in developing an employment brand strategy, which helped double employee growth in six years.

Libby shared her thoughts on leadership, women in the workplace, balancing work and family, and career development.

- I believe you serve those you lead by giving them the tools, knowledge, and mentorship they need to get their jobs done. Forming good relationships above you, on the same level with you, and below you is how people succeed in the workplace. This is accomplished by thinking about what others need, not what you need.

- I'm nice *and* I have a corner office. The challenges that women face in the workplace are different from what I faced almost thirty years ago. My group's challenge was that we were the first generation of women who actually had the same goals and dreams for our careers as men, and we walked right into the "old boys' network." Today's generation of women (and I am speaking about this not only as a human resources executive, but as the mother of a twenty-two-year-old woman) is faced with a different reality. The law schools, the MBA programs, and the med schools are all fifty-fifty, women and men. So when "it" [gender differences in the workplace] comes at them, they don't recognize it and are completely blindsided. I think as time goes on, "it" will become less and less of an issue.

- Some of the problems stem from attitude and outlook. Don't look for discrimination from bosses, peers, coworkers, and subordinates. As you go up the rungs, sometimes you need to be a little quieter and listen and learn. When situations arise, I ask myself if it was because I am a woman, but generally I see the same challenges for men at the highest levels. People always point to the absence of women CEOs as proof that women are discriminated against in the workplace. I have a different view. I think of all the senior executive women I know, I don't know too many who want to be CEOs. I think that women who have children realize that being a CEO is often too much to take on.

- Women and men have the same hopes and dreams coming into the workplace. Most people come to work every day wanting to give their best, to give value and add value. And they want to know that if they deliver what is expected of them, they will get something in return.

be honest: your strengths and weaknesses as a leader

According to Hay's study by the global experts on organizational clarity, people capabilities, and employee commitment, trust and confidence in top leadership was the single most reliable predictor of employee satisfaction in an organization. So to keep happy and productive people, you must continually evaluate your strengths and weaknesses as a leader. We used the findings from the study to create the following checklist:

- **Do you communicate the company's overall business strategy to employees?** Make sure each department knows how their goals move the entire operation forward. It's important for senior managers to interact with all levels of the operation. Employees need to feel part of the bigger goal of an organization; otherwise, they are easily distracted and disinterested in their tasks. This is especially true of new members of the workforce who have a number of individual tasks and not entire projects to accomplish.
- **Do you communicate how the employees' contributions help achieve key business objectives?** Employees want constant communication, especially about how their efforts help the organization succeed. Create systems for communicating good news with individuals, departments, and the entire company. Many large corporations have established company intranet sets for intracompany communication. Information is shared between departments, and employees are even encouraged to blog about their activities.
- **Do you share information on both how the company is doing and how an employee's own division is doing?** Employees, especially ones who own company stock as part of their

retirement or pension plans, have a vested interest in the company's success and want regular reports.

· **Do you know your own job inside and out and have a solid familiarity with your employees' tasks?** As a manager you have a responsibility to lead by example.

· **Do you search for ways to guide your organization to new heights?** A leader's most important role is to move the business to the next level.

· **When things go wrong, do you analyze the situation, fix it, and move on to the next challenge, avoiding placing the blame on others or disruptively holding on to past issues?** Placing blame is the fastest way to lose the confidence of the team. We've heard it again and again in our interviews—bad bosses are blamers. The number two no-no, by the way, is taking credit for the team's work. As the leader you need to take pride in the accomplishments of your team. After all, if they succeed, you succeed.

· **Do you make sound and timely decisions, making sure to meet deadlines for your staff?** The worst thing you can do is hold the team up because you are too busy to give timely feedback.

· **Are you a good role model for your employees?** You can't just tell them what to do; they must see you doing it. Of course, there is a flip side to this too; they had better not see you acting badly, either.

· **Do you care about your employees' well-being and job satisfaction?** You'd better.

· **Do you work with your team to develop good work habits and a sense of responsibility?** Don't take for granted that the team understands what ownership of a task means.

· **Do you make sure that subordinates understand what they are supposed to accomplish and know how to get the tasks**

done? Subordinates need the big picture and the nitty-gritty. Don't overlook that.

- **Do you operate as a team and not just a bunch of individuals doing their respective jobs?** Truly operating as a team takes time and effort. Managers need to evaluate the strengths and weaknesses of each team member, then figure out a game plan to get the most productivity from the group.

are you using the full capabilities of your organization?

According to Meredith Belbin, author of *Management Teams: Why They Succeed or Fail*, there are nine team roles and we all carry out one or more functions. The key to a good, efficient team is to create a healthy balance of these individuals or to identify the roles that you need your team members to play even if that's not their natural role.

Belbin's nine team roles are:

The Plant
Original thinkers; they generate new ideas; they offer solutions to problems; they think in radically different ways, laterally, imaginatively.

The Resource Investigator
They are creative; they like to take ideas and run with them; they are extroverted and popular.

The Coordinator
Highly disciplined and controlled; they can focus on objectives; they unify a team.

The Shaper

Very achievement oriented; they like to be challenged and get re-sults.

The Monitor Evaluator

Analyze and balance and weigh; they are calm and detached; they are objective thinkers.

The Team Worker

Supportive and cooperative; they make good diplomats because they want only what is best for the team.

The Implementer

Good organizational skills; they display common sense; they like to get the job done.

The Completer

They check details; they tidy up after themselves; they are painstakingly conscientious.

The Specialist

Dedicated to acquiring a specialized skill; they are extremely pro-fessional; they have drive and dedication.

At YC Media, our boutique public relations company, we look for "shapers." We need highly motivated publicists who want to achieve results. We also need them to exhibit "completer" skills, so we have created systems that force the shapers to "sweat the details."

the mistakes women make: sometimes it's harder being a girl

Is there a woman manager whom you really admire? A boss who has always been supportive and fair, shepherding you through every step of your career, teaching, coaching, and then promoting you up the ranks? We didn't have one either. Excellent bosses are rare and excellent female bosses are rarer still. We're not selling out the sisterhood here. There's a double standard in the workplace. What's okay for a man is most definitely not okay for a woman. Over and over in our interviews we heard the same thing: "I'd much rather work for a man; women are too emotional." Sarilee Norton, president of Tru-Tech Business for Temple Inland, summed it up best: "A man can rant and rave and they say he's angry. A woman can rant and rave and they say she's crazy. If they can dismiss you as crazy, they don't have to pay attention to the issue."

Try to identify a role model in your company and follow in her footsteps. We've had bosses who were obviously brilliant, creative, and talented people. They ran teams, small and large, and we wanted to work hard for them each day. Yet even with all of their obvious talents and successes, we always felt they could have done more to inspire and support their staff. After spending just a couple of hours on the Internet researching leadership training for women, we were shocked to find that most of the female mentors, or even virtual mentors, were older white women wearing sensible shoes and suits. The advice they offer to young women going to their first job interview sounds like bad Emily Post: "When you meet someone new, a first impression is made in the first thirty seconds. You'll want to pay attention to everything you can control in those thirty seconds, such as your attire, poise, etiquette, eye contact, voice, and handshake. Try to convey professionalism and warmth. As for your attire, remember that dressing for success never goes out of style! Stand tall, and always shake hands and introduce yourself. Make your handshake a complete and firm grip. Be sure to maintain eye contact (as opposed to gazing at the door or the ceiling, which can happen when you're nervous). Looking people in the eye conveys confidence and openness. Pay attention to how you sit in a chair, how you cross your legs (at the ankle is best, if at all), and how you hold your hands (in your lap). Your poise is part of your package. How is your voice? A soft voice makes others have to work too hard to listen. On the other hand, a loud voice can come on too strong. Many people lower or speed up their voices when they are anxious. Be aware of your tendencies."

Is she kidding? "Your poise is part of your package." We stopped listening right there. Of course your poise is important, but would you say it that way? Were our mothers and grandmothers fighting for us to go to college and get jobs we enjoy so we could be forced into sensible shoes and rayon business suits? We hope not. Nothing about that conveys leadership. Our vision of leadership allows individuals to be themselves while working for the greater good of the group. Of course, a corporate culture comes into play; however, it should be possible to be a good leader and still maintain your own identity.

leaders, know thyself: personality traits and tests

No one would describe us as company girls, so when the women we interviewed presented us with corporate jargon and acronyms, we did some homework. We found that personality tests are widely given in job interviews, career counseling centers, and at management training seminars. The results are supposed to help you know yourself better so you can flex your management style for those with varied personalities; you're taught to adapt your style as different situations require. We were generally skeptical of this kind of thing until one of our colleagues told us a story. An executive at a fast-growing company, she was feeling overwhelmed with the management challenges that her expanding staff presented. She requested some management training and was sent off-site to a one-day seminar. Upon entering the seminar, the group was given the Myers-Briggs Type Indicator. Developed by Katherine Briggs and her daughter Isabel Briggs Myers and based on Swiss psychologist Carl Jung's studies on psychological type, the MBTI scale is made up of four basic categories, each of which has two opposite poles. People generally "lean toward" one pole or the other either moderately or, in some cases, quite strongly. From this fundamental division eight psychological "preferences" and sixteen personality "types" emerge. Management consultants use the test results to predict behavior. For example, extremely extroverted people have to understand that when an introverted member of their team doesn't stand up and cheer for a job well done that they are not being disrespectful, they are just not comfortable standing up and cheering. For a free personality test online, visit www.ustechnicaljobs.com. You will have to sign up for their referral service, but it's well worth it for a quick and free test.

EXTRAVERSION-INTROVERSION

The first preferences measured by the Myers-Briggs test relate to how we deal with the outside world. Extraverts (E) are energized by having interactions with others and may often speak without thinking something through. They are people of action and present their best abilities to the world. Introverts (I) prefer quiet reflection and may think about something and never get to the point of telling others. They keep their best skills to themselves, and present their secondary skills to others.

SENSING-INTUITION

The next set of preferences, sensing-intuition differences affect how we take in and process data. Sensors (S) gather information through experiences and are practical and orderly. Intuitors (N) gather information through relationships and concepts—picking things up by watching, grasping ideas before getting to grips with details.

THINKING-FEELING

The Thinking-Feeling differences affect how we make decisions. Thinkers (T) make decisions objectively and impersonally using logic. Feelers (F) make decisions subjectively and personally based on what they feel is "right." A Thinker will tend to decide things based on logic, while a Feeler will base it more on their emotions and the feelings of others. It is interesting that, in the United States at least, about 67 percent of all men are Thinkers, while 67 percent of females are Feelers.

JUDGING-PERCEIVING

Finally, Judging-Perceiving differences affect how we prefer to live. Judgers (J) like being planned and structured and having things settled and decided. Perceivers (P) like being spontaneous, unstructured, open, and flexible.

It all sounds too complicated until we return to our friend's management training class. After the trainees answered a series of questions and the results were scored, the group was divided into Judgers and Perceivers and asked to plan a vacation. The Perceivers chose a tropical island vacation and filled their days with activities and their nights with social events. Each day was chock-full of options for fun and relaxation. The Perceivers, however, neglected to choose a date or plan how they were getting to their destination. The Judgers in contrast decided when they were going, how they were getting there right down to airport transfers, but neglected to choose a place where they wanted to be. Amazing. Two groups of similarly successful professionals with polar opposite views of the world. What became apparent to them (and us) was that if you have an indication of a person's traits, you can support their natural weaknesses. Another colleague, Amie Malkin, the managing director of health care for Burson-Marsteller in London, is an ESTJ—an extraverted, practical, objective, and structured person. Her reviews most commonly recommend that she offer "more carrot, less stick." For her, knowing this about herself has enabled her to have more patience with people and be more supportive and less directive.

To check this out for ourselves, we went online and took the free personality test at www.ustechnicaljobs.com. Here's what it said:

Kim scored as an ENFP (Extravert, Intuitive, Feeler, Perceiver). ENFPs tend to be enthusiastic, talkative, and outgoing; clever, curious, and playful; deeply caring, sensitive, and gentle; highly innovative, creative, optimistic, and unique; adaptable and resourceful but sometimes disorganized. The most important thing to ENFPs is freedom to see possibilities, make connections, and be with a variety of people.

Caitlin is an ISFJ (Introvert, Sensor, Feeler, Judger). ISFJs tend to be cautious, gentle, and thoughtful; hesitant until they know people well, then affectionate and caring; very literal and aware of the physical world; uncompromising about personal standards and easily offended; diligent and conscientious, organized and decisive. The most important thing to ISFJs is living a stable, predictable life and helping people in real ways.

Clearly the quiz has deemed us opposite types, but in such a way that our personalities are complementary, and in fact beneficial to our working relationship. For instance, Kim's ability to be continually outgoing and talkative enables her to keep up with the busy social aspect of running a PR firm, and Caitlin's receptive and thoughtful nature positions her well to manage the team and deal with sensitive situations. In our case, the sum is most definitely greater than the two parts.

girl talk

COURTNEY LYNCH AND ANGELA MORGAN

Courtney and Angela are founders of Lead Star, a leadership training company that presents dynamic, energetic workshops that focus on developing and discovering the natural leadership traits women possess. On their Web site (www.leadingfromthe front.com), Courtney and Angela describe themselves in terms of their roles. Courtney describes herself as a "leader, wife, daughter, friend, and lawyer" and Angie describes herself as a "leader, wife, mother, volunteer, and employee." One role missing in their description was Marine. Both joined the Marine Corps while in college in the ROTC (Reserve Officer Training Corps) program. They graduated as officers and began their service commanding platoons of fifty soldiers at the ages of twenty-two and twenty-three. Both in the way they lead their lives and in the lessons they teach, the Marine Corps has had a profound impact on their lives. It is their belief that leadership skills can be used in all of the roles women play in their lives. A stay-at-home mom needs leadership skills to calm the chaos, a daughter needs leadership skills to care for an aging parent, and a manager needs leadership skills to get a good result from her team. At Lead Star, they define a leader as one who influences outcomes and inspires others. We spoke to them about their leadership training and their philosophy, "Lead as you are. Always."

How did being in the Marine Corps prepare you to be great leaders and train others in leadership?
The Marine Corps gave us all the tools we needed to lead—from practical leadership principles and character traits to rigorous

training in environments where we were encouraged to succeed, even though failure as we developed was allowed. Thus, once we got to the "real world," we were proven leaders. The Marine Corps has been training leaders for 230 years—their methods have withstood the test of time. In the Marine Corps and at Lead Star, leadership is not about being complex, it's about being effective. Not only did the Marine Corps give us great training, it gave us great opportunities to apply the skills we learned. Our leadership skills focused on taking care of others, and as Marine officers we were immediately tasked with that. In the private sector it would take many years to achieve that level of management/leadership experience.

Do you think there are differences between the skills needed for great women leaders vs. men leaders?

Strong leadership skills transcend gender. All leaders must have integrity, take initiative, have sound judgment, and take care of those they lead. While the skills are the same, leadership styles are personal and individualized. We all have different strengths and weaknesses (and some may be compatible with our gender), but regardless, we have to recognize them and overcome them in our efforts to be the best leader possible.

Studies have shown that to be effective leaders, women and men have to lead differently. Was this your experience in the Marine Corps? If so, can you describe the differences?

We think every individual needs to lead differently. Women don't need to take on masculine personas to be strong leaders. We learned this early on. One of our few female officers (1,000 out of 180,000 Marines are female officers) was a very nice woman with an odd quirk. Whenever she was in front of her troops or in front of men, she adopted a manly persona. She lowered her voice, changed her posture, and ultimately forfeited her credibility. She also recommended to Courtney that if she wanted to succeed in the Marine Corps, that she had to do the same. Courtney was conflicted. As this woman was the commanding officer, Courtney was supposed to follow her orders, but while appreciating that she was trying to help, Courtney also strongly disagreed with her. Ironically enough, what saved Courtney was a crusty old colonel, a stereo-typical Marine. He called Courtney into his office and without ac-knowledging what was happening with the commanding officer he told her that she needed to lead as who she was. He said, "Being a leader is not about playing a part, but being credible and being yourself, and if you don't lead as you are, you will never earn the respect of those you command."

Our takeaway from the Marine Corps is that while good lead-ers share consistent traits, they exhibit them in many different ways. We've worked for great leaders who were shy, who were boisterous, who were stoic, and who were warm. Personality plays a big role in your leadership style.

What are the three most important traits (skills) women should learn to be great leaders?
Integrity, decisiveness, and courage—courage to take risks, to make a change, and even to fail.

How do you manage to be a strong leader without being labeled a bitch?
The strongest leaders display compassion and a sense of service to others. Poor leaders get caught up in the notoriety of their position or the power and prestige a title brings. Those are the leaders who are likely to be labeled a bitch because they have defined leader-ship to mean something about them instead of about those they lead.

As a leader you must be confident. The easiest way to be con-fident is to be competent. The Marines taught us the importance of "leading from the front." The Marines encourage you to continually take initiative; however, you must set standards that you can meet. When Courtney was a Marine, she carried a 9mm pistol. She had never touched a gun before joining the Marines and wasn't a par-ticularly skilled shot. The Marines in the platoon she commanded were required to qualify on a large rifle, an M-16 to be exact, and so she had to meet that standard also. It wasn't easy, but she did it. Leaders meet the standards they ask of others. In the private sector, an obvious example of leading from the front is with the

8:00 a.m. meeting. If the leader calls the meeting, then the leader needs to meet the standard and be there on time. Too often managers will call an 8:00 a.m. meeting and then saunter in at 8:15. It's disrespectful to the people who have been waiting for you and undermines your ability to lead.

We've found that as women we're not immediately accepted as leaders. How do we earn this critical buy-in?

Performance is the key to gaining buy-in and respect. Respect is what you should aspire to as a leader. You shouldn't strive to have people like you, but it is critical for them to respect you. We both agree that as women or as any minority in an organization you are likely going to have to prove yourself more often than the majority, but if you are a consistent performer, eventually your positive reputation will build. As Marines, we often felt the responsibility of our entire gender. We weren't just acting as Courtney and Angie, but as women, and we took the responsibility seriously. We limited socializing with our Marines to a minimum and Courtney even adopted a "no-dating Marines" policy. [Luckily, Angie didn't go that far, as she dated and ultimately married a Marine—one who, she was quick to point out, "was not in her chain of command."]

What do you think are the biggest leadership mistakes women make? What are the biggest mistakes that men make?

Women often confuse leadership with a popularity contest. Leading can be lonely. You are entrusted with responsibility and the opportunity to influence outcomes and inspire others. The need to make tough decisions for the good of the whole team often leads to dissatisfaction among individuals. Women tend to internalize this dissatisfaction more than they should. Accept the reality and move on.

Men struggle with compassion and communication skills more often than women. When you lack compassion, you have a hard time anticipating the needs of your team and addressing them. This can ultimately hurt your efforts to build camaraderie and a sense of common purpose. Weak communication skills allow minor issues to become major issues.

Many women we interviewed have said that it is much easier for them to work for male bosses. Was this your experience in the Marine Corps and do you have any thoughts on why this would be the case?

We have more experience with men in leadership roles. Yet with the emphasis on leadership skills in the Corps, we almost became gender blind, male or female became a moot point—we just recognized the positive differences of working for leaders. When we've had a hard time working for a woman or a man, it's likely because the person we are working for is not a leader. It's really not easier to work for a man. It's just easier to work for a leader.

How does leading from the front differ from other leadership styles?

Leaders who lead from the front continuously take initiative and make decisions. They also meet or exceed the standards they expect others to meet. Leaders keep making decisions in order to keep making progress. The Corps taught us the "80 percent solution," that a good decision today is better than a great decision tomorrow. And procrastination is a decision all on its own.

There's so much conflicting information out there. Entire books are written on the premise that "nice girls don't get promoted" and "win like a man." How do we become strong, empowered, inspiring women without acting like men?

There is a wide variety of information out there, but the heart of being an effective leader is understanding who you are and leading as you are. You've got to be credible in order to inspire others. That's why we started Lead Star. We wanted to inspire and empower women to lead as they are—we are proof positive that staying true to yourself is the key to being an authentic, capable leader. When you lead as you are, you don't ignore your weaknesses—you always have to be working to improve—but you learn how to compensate for them with your strengths.

three

team building

YOU'RE ONLY AS GOOD AS YOUR STAFF

One of the more nonnegotiable facts of business life is that in order to succeed as a leader, you need a solid team supporting you. Your employees are only as good as you select and develop them, so in addition to your overall goals, you need to always be focused on building and nurturing a team of hard workers you can trust and rely on.

Whether creating a team from scratch or supporting one that you've "inherited," assembling the right mix of people is essential to the smooth operation of your company, team, division, or unit.

From hiring and training new members to winning the loyalty of the old-timers, we'll tell you what you need to know and do to create an environment in which team members—from assistants to associates—will flourish.

evaluating your peeps: do you have the team you want?

Whether you hired them yourself or they came with your new position, you need to periodically evaluate your team. Our preferred method of doing this is with an Org (short for *organizational*) Chart. An Org Chart is an illustration of the inner structure of a business or, in this case, your team. It is a presentation of the relationships within the team, identified by lines of authority. When you fill in your Org Chart with names and titles, it makes it easy to visualize the inner structure of the group, and will make it easier to see holes in the staff or redundancies in responsibilities.

An Org Chart looks something like this:

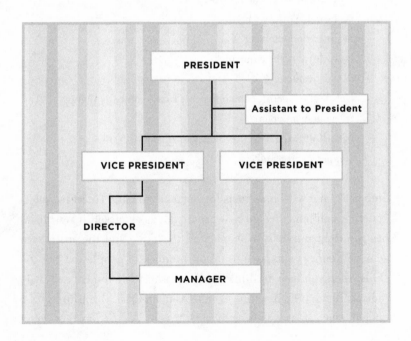

Create an Org Chart like this one, listing the names of your employees and leaving space next to each name for the following information:

- Title
- Salary
- Date of hire
- Date of last review
- Date of last raise
- Date of last promotion

Answer the following questions as best you can for each employee:

- Is she expecting a raise and/or promotion?
- What are her responsibilities?
- Is she delegating correctly?
- Is she a good manager?
- Is she loyal to the company?
- Is she loyal to me?
- How is she "feeling" about her role in the company (happy, frustrated, anxious)?
- Is she following both the unspoken and spoken rules of the company and team?

Step back, and with your goals for the team in hand (increase sales, generate publicity, design new products), ask yourself if your team has the right number of people and the skills and the attitude to achieve them. If you have the right number of people but not the skills, then you have to think about retraining. If you have an attitude problem, then it is time to address it, and fast. If you don't have enough staff, then it is time to hire. If your boss is hesitant about adding to the payroll, get ready to make your case. Write up a job description, outline the reasons why it isn't possible for existing employees to fill the gap, and remember to demonstrate how this new hire is going to improve profitability down the road.

SIGNS THAT YOUR EMPLOYEE MAY BE GETTING READY TO JUMP SHIP

- Mysterious appointments during the day always alluded to in vague terms.
- Your Grateful Dead–loving assistant shows up for work dressed like a bank teller.
- Every time you approach the printer, she rushes past you to snatch the pile of paper (résumés!) sitting in the tray.
- When you are within five feet of the employee's desk, she begins frantically closing Word documents.
- More than once a day you look out the window and see your employee on the sidewalk, talking on her cell phone.
- You can't quite put your finger on it, but your employee has developed a bit of a 'tude.
- When you assign a complex project to the employee, she doesn't ask follow-up questions.

the right fit: making the good hire

So, based on the Org Chart and the goals you have been hired to achieve, do you have the people to get it done? Once you're up to speed on the legalities of hiring (see page 54), then you can start looking. But whom do you hire? Where do you find them? How do you determine if they are right for you?

WHO?

Before calling human resources or placing an ad, work out on paper what you need in an employee. This includes a list of desired skills, a salary range, and a rough idea of personality traits you think would mesh well with the existing group, especially the person to whom they will report. Also, write out a complete job description so you can articulate with accuracy what the daily, weekly, and monthly responsibilities will be.

Anat Baron, entrepreneur, reminds us that while we might be looking for someone familiar, there are benefits to thinking broader. "I am a big believer in diversity. Not just the normal ethnic, cultural kind, but diversity of ideas. I think teams work best when you mix people up. Different backgrounds and work experience. They challenge each other. The common interest becomes getting the job done."

WHERE?

If you've been promoted to a supervisory position in a company or corporation, your human resources department may have a policy of promoting from within, or of handling the first stage of the recruitment process, so make your contact there your first stop.

If your business does not have an HR department, then it's your responsibility to get the word out. Depending on the level of the employee, you could take out an ad in the local paper, check in with career counselors at local colleges, register with Web sites such as Monster.com or Careerbuilder.com, find a reputable headhunter by asking your colleagues for a name or by checking out the classifieds in a trade magazine, and/or e-mail people in your professional circle. Recently we sent an e-mail to our network asking for help finding an account executive (a mid-level associate in a public relations agency). Within days, our e-mail was dispersed to what seemed like hundreds of people and we began receiving résumés from friends,

friends of friends, and friends of friends of friends. Since we were very specific about the skill set we sought, most of the referrals we received were legitimate candidates.

The one caveat worth noting about going to your personal network for job candidates is that, as we stated in our first book, you should stay away from considering or hiring friends, family, ex-bosses, ex-assistants, and ex-boyfriends or -girlfriends. You want working relationships to be as baggage-free as possible.

HOW?

Interviewing, interviewing, and more interviewing, and trusting your gut. Even if HR sends you someone they've billed as the "perfect" candidate, if your instincts are signaling Danger Ahead, then approach with extreme caution. Ask lots of direct questions. Maybe even explain your concerns to a peer at the company and ask her to interview the person and give you a second opinion. It's our firm belief that if you sense a problem, there may be one there, even if only in the chemistry between you and the potential employee.

Now, many people will tell you that you don't have to like an employee. If a quirky employee does an excellent job, then that should be enough. That may be true if she works in the London office while you're in, say, Los Angeles, or if she's on the road most of the time. But if you have to see this person and interact with her daily, or even weekly, it would make life a lot more pleasant if you liked her too.

Stephanie Teuwen, president of Teuwen One Image, says, "Once the skills have been established in the interview, then it's all about personality. It's a bit like dating! You need to get along well and be a team." But don't hire someone just because you like them. About a year ago we were looking to hire a junior account executive to help us run the office while learning the business. The ideal candidate would come with a little professional experience and a lot of enthusiasm for public relations. We interviewed a great person who we had a ton in common with on a personal level. She was smart and fun to be around, but when we asked her why she was interested in working for us, she said "because I figured it is time for me to have a real job." While we liked her, we just couldn't trust that she got what it meant to work in a professional office environment and we didn't have the time or energy to bring her up to speed on the basics.

a note for entrepreneurs: before you hire

For those who own their own business, hiring an employee is a *very* big deal. You are sometimes doubling your payroll with just one employee, and when you double your company, even on a small scale, the entire dynamic of your business changes. Before inviting someone to join the business, have the employee manual done, the payroll set up, the job responsibilities outlined, and most importantly, work out for yourself the expectations you have for this employee. When you know exactly what you want and need from a new employee, you'll be able to communicate clearly from day one.

legalities of hiring

If there are holes that need to be filled, before you even think about calling a headhunter or taking out an ad, Laurie Malkin, an employment lawyer at Schulte Roth & Zabel LLP, has a few key pieces of hiring advice: "Don't assume that you're an expert on employment law just because you're the boss and good at what you do for a living. Do you have any idea how many different laws govern or relate to the employment relationship? For New York City employers, for instance, the number is at least forty-five. Without proper legal advice when you're hiring employees, it is unlikely that you'll know things such as what types of questions applicable antidiscrimination laws prohibit; when the law requires you to pay a new employee overtime; and whether and, if so, how to conduct pre-employment medical examinations or drug tests." If you don't have the funds to hire a lawyer and you are without a human resource director to help you navigate the legal waters, then it is time to spend some quality time on the Internet. Laurie tells us that federal, state, and local government agencies all have detailed Web sites that provide guidance about hiring and firing in compliance with the applicable law. They are easy to find. Two good places to start are www.dol.gov, the official site of the U.S. Department of Labor, and www.eeoc.gov, the official site of the U.S. Equal Employment Opportunity Commission.

interviewing

When chatting with a potential candidate, keep in mind the spoken and unspoken rules of your work environment—the company culture—and share important details with candidates you think have potential. Are there several out-of-town conferences that the employee will be expected to attend? Though the "official" office hours are nine to six, can most employees nonetheless be found at their desks on Sunday afternoon? If there is an expectation of long hours, it is only fair to prepare the candidate. Also factor in the "personality" of the office. Let's say that your group is highly productive but conservative and relatively humorless; in that case, it might not be fair to anyone if you hired a high-energy, high-strung, artsy candidate. Stephanie Teuwen shares that, "Aside from figuring out if the potential employee has the required skills or transferable skills, my number one priority is their personality. Will they fit in our environment, be happy, complement the team, and enjoy our clients? I really try to see their soul and their heart without asking inappropriate questions. When I feel that the person is a potential 'go,' I have him or her meet the rest of the team for a casual discussion, and we regroup the following day to share our experience. Nobody would be hired if my team didn't like them. We're like a small family; we need to 'adopt' the new member together."

Ask yourself if you think a potential employee would be happy as a part of the group. It might be difficult for you yourself to make this call, especially if the candidate is yessing you, so consider setting up interviews with a few key team members, including the potential employee's direct report.

Be honest about the job and the amount of grunt work required. You don't want them balking every time they are asked to file a piece of paper. If they are a newbie to your industry and the reality is that they will be spending the first couple of years running errands, do them a favor and give them a heads-up. We have had people turn our job offers down because they didn't like hearing that we were going to ask them to stuff a lot of gift bags. Sure, it was a drag to keep interviewing, but it would have been a bigger drag to work with a bitter assistant.

If the candidate is between jobs, this is a perfect opportunity for you to test one another out. Bring them in for a week to work with you and the rest of the team. You won't learn everything about them in five days, but you will be witness to hopefully their highest quality of work as they try to win the job. If their best isn't good enough for you, then at least you found that out before you offered them a job.

no head games and power trips during the interview, please

You know when you won't learn a single thing about a potential candidate? When you are treating the interview as an opportunity to play *Big Bad Boss*. When Leigh Ann, a friend of ours, arrived at a public relations company for an internship interview, she was shown to an empty office with a single desk and a single chair. The owner came in and placed a pen on the table; she then handed Leigh Ann a piece of paper and a pencil. "I want you to write a paragraph that will inspire a journalist to write about this pen." When she returned and picked up the "test," she shook her head and said "absolutely wrong." She went on to explain that our friend was supposed to "sell the pen" to journalists. Something a college senior with no experience in public relations would never have known. Bottom line—it didn't make sense, and only served to make the candidate feel inferior and clam up.

To learn the most from a potential candidate, make her feel comfortable. Remember to smile when you greet her, ask her if she found the office okay, offer her water, and spend the first few minutes chatting. Before jumping in on the tough questions, start with the lighter ones. You might ask an entry-level candidate what her favorite class was in school or a more senior person how she found themselves in the industry. But don't start off an interview with a question about why she left her last job. The point is to not challenge her right away so that she is not in defensive mode throughout the interview.

if you teach them: how to train effectively

Wouldn't it be a perfect world if you could just tell someone what needs to get done and never give it another thought? Or better yet, if you didn't have to say anything at all because your employee had ESP and was a self-starting perfectionist? Alas, chances are just about zero that you will lead a training-free existence and, in fact, it is actually one of your most important job requirements.

Everyone seems to agree that the most effective way to train is to make taking the time to do it right a priority and recognizing that the individuals on your staff need a different level of guidance from you. As discussed in chapter 2, this situation leadership style is recognizing that various levels of staff needed a different type of management from you. Junior staff members are still developing into professionals and so need your help cultivating the basics of office etiquette, as well as the nuts and bolts of actually performing their duties. Senior people shouldn't need to be schooled in the basics of professionalism or how to do their job, but do need you to express your vision and what their role in attaining it is.

Adrienne Arsht, chairman of the board of TotalBank in Miami, recommends setting up the ground rules early with new senior employees: "I would sit down and talk directly about your own management style: This is what I mean when I say this or that. I respect you, that's why I hired you; so if I come off rude, it isn't personal. When you hear something you don't like, come and talk to me about it directly."

With both junior and senior staff members, consider establishing a mentor system within your team. Develop a few people on all levels to become mentors for all new employees. They need to know the company inside and out, be enthusiastic about being there, work well with you, and be a positive spokesperson for both the company and you. When a junior-level employee starts, partner him up with a peer so he becomes the point person for ongoing office questions (Where do I find pens? What is the policy on lunch? Where is the nearest bank?).

The early stages of training an employee are a delicate and crucial time. You want to teach him to take responsibility for his work and himself while showing that you are supportive. Tammy Blake, a senior level manager at a publishing house, told us about scheduling a First Day for new employees that will at least point them in the direction of achieving success at your company.

sample first-day plan for new employee

- Breakfast with you (and their direct report if that isn't you)
- Introduction to team mentor
- Team mentor brings new employee around the company for casual introductions
- Lunch with team mentor
- Afternoon with direct report to go over upcoming week's schedule

your gal friday: do you need an assistant and what should she be like?

Your assistant, almost more than any other member of your team, represents you to the outside world. In many cases, she is the first person that your professional network encounters en route to see you. Because she usually answers your phone and greets your guests, you want this assistant to shine. There is a very famous chef in our circle who had a kick-ass assistant. She was always responsive, pleasant, and professional. She knew where the chef was at all times and was able to get answers, confirm VIP reservations, and set up photo shoots on a quick turnaround. When she moved on, this chef hired a new assistant who did none of the above. Because, like most niche industries, the food world is so tiny, everyone was talking about this hiring misstep. Jokes were made, media opportunities were lost (because she couldn't or wouldn't get answers fast enough), and eventually she lost her job. And the chef? He lost a lot of face. What's the lesson here? Take a long hard look at your current assistant. Are you comfortable having her speak for you? Ask a few outside colleagues for a candid appraisal of what their experience with your assistant has been like.

When filling this position, make sure you have enough work to fill her day. Unlike other staff positions, an assistant is almost entirely dependent on you to assign tasks and responsibilities on an almost daily basis. When interviewing, make sure there is a rapport, that she exudes confidence, dresses appropriately, and is polite. Avoid the pit bulls; they really don't make you look good, even if they can block your doorway from unwelcome guests. Hire someone who has shown loyalty to other bosses, because you don't want your assistant to become the source of office gossip. Because if the assistant is disloyal to you, or not a very professional person, she will tell the staff if you are having problems with your husband, when you scoot out for a manicure, and whenever you are called upstairs. You can assess loyalty during the interview by asking her the best and worst things about her previous manager. Look at her résumé to see how long she kept each job and see if she listed any of her direct reports as references.

And remember what Patti LaBelle told Caitlin as they were boarding a plane together during a book tour: Your assistant must "always, always, always represent."

good witch

A REALLY GOOD WITCH
Here's a story from our friend Amy Curry:

My best female boss, Jackie, was someone who over the course of a working relationship managed to help me develop self-confidence, in which I was sorely lacking. She did this without the intention of mentoring or changing me. It was mostly an outcome of who she was as a boss and a person.

In thinking back, I guess the reasons for it working so well for me came down to several things, including

- *her belief that everyone on her team had something valuable to offer (hierarchy wasn't important; ideas were)*
- *her ability to delegate responsibilities and her trust that the task will get done*
- *her lack of need to micromanage*
- *her personality*

She managed to pull together a team that had complementary skills so that everyone had their own responsibilities and domain. She respected everyone's voice and opinions and encouraged ideas. Remarkably, she did not take disagreements as a sign of disrespect. Instead, she saw them as commitment to the idea and passion for the project. She and I would often have "heated" discussions about the work we were involved in, and through it, we learned a tremendous amount from each other and were able to arrive at some conclusion. Nothing was taken personally because the discussion really focused on articulating the ideas, and trying to see whose background and powers of persuasion were most able to move the ideas forward.

In my case being valued for what I could do, and being given the responsibilities, was truly important. Mostly, the fact that she appreciated the work, and was not threatened by it (because she and I had a very different professional background and skills), was liberating. Although there was a structure, she was the PI (principal investigator of the project) and I was slowly promoted to project manager over time. What worked best for me was the fact that there was less formal hierarchy in the working atmosphere.

Finally, Jackie had no interest in micromanaging the project, which meant that we would check in about our workload and deadlines and discuss what our plans for completing the work were, but then, how and when we did it was up to us. For me, what works best is this more flexible type of goal-setting. This implies trust. I say I am going to get something done, my boss trusts that I will, and doesn't therefore manage the little steps to getting there.

All these things are critical, but I think most critical to the success in this work relationship was the way in which our personalities and work styles matched. Though we don't work together anymore, we still meet for lunch as friends. We had a natural connection in style and outlook.

We think that Amy's boss Jackie was a Good Witch for sure. She seemed to have done everything right, starting with the golden rule of management: Respect your people and respect yourself. She demonstrated respect by "encouraging ideas" and soliciting input and opinions. She had faith in their abilities by stepping back and not "micromanaging." She took her ego out of it and focused on "moving ideas forward." Wow.

handling old loyalties: was your predecessor cooler than you?

It is scary to inherit an employee, let alone a whole team. Think about when a new manager was hired over you. What emotions did it bring up? You were most likely anxious that she would want to replace you. Resentful that you had to prove yourself all over again.

Distrustful of the direction she was going to take the group. Unsettled by the change, defensive about your contribution and your right to be there, and even nostalgic about the way things used to be. And let's be honest: There might even have been a small part of you that wanted to see her fail.

Now turn it around and this is the emotional landscape that you are now managing. Truth be told, you have to prove yourself worthy of your employees' loyalty, hard work, and respect. This is even more challenging if your predecessor was adored. Everyone we interviewed said the same thing, "take it slow." Unless you have an employee who is blatantly undermining you, try not to fire anyone right away. You want to spend the first few weeks watching and listening. Here is a trick: Assess the team you have been given, and identify the leader in the group. This is the person who inspires those around them (even at a junior level) and who many turn to with questions. This is someone you want on your side. Beware of the ones that are most solicitous; they are not who you need right now, but rather the corporate equivalent of the trendsetter. You want them to make respecting and listening to you the latest trend. If they are not on your side, then make it your mission to turn it around. Because of their power in the group, they can undermine your authority.

People are going to fear you, so use this to your advantage by maintaining professional distance (don't go out to lunch with the team unless you initiate it, avoid the watercooler chitchat, skip the drinks after work), and don't fall into the trap of wanting everyone to like you. Unfortunately, it seems like women have more challenges in this area than men. Beth Kramer, a VP of New Product Development, tells us, "I think the biggest problem with employees I inherited is they didn't see the need to listen to me or pay attention—there were gender issues here, and also issues around differences in academic degrees and work experience. Because our organization was strongly collaborative and consensus driven, I couldn't simply say 'because I said so.' "

If your team wasn't prepared for your arrival or promotion, it can also make for a rocky transition, as was the case when Ayelet Baron, Anat's sister, was hired. "The first challenge was they were not told about the changes by their management team until the last minute. And when they were told about it, the vision for the change was never shared with them, so we started off with a very tense environment. They had lost their trust in management looking out for their needs and were suspicious of the new management." To make things worse for Ayelet, "when I asked the former manager about the performance of each person on his team (I didn't know most of them), he failed to mention that one of them got a poor rating on his last review. And when I inherited this group of people, I found out that most of the internal clients didn't want him working on their projects. Everyone on the team liked him but knew that he was the weakest link. I had to spend a lot of time giving him a new assignment and working closely on performance expectations. This took a lot of time and energy away from forming the new team."

So what to do? Step back, evaluate your team, and be very clear about who you are and what you have been hired to do. A great opportunity to do this is during the one-on-one meetings you are going to set up with your senior team members. Show that you want to do whatever you can to help them succeed in their careers, outline the vision you have been given for the company, and whatever you do, don't start out the discussion by introducing sweeping changes. Remember that the most successful transitions are those that begin and end with honesty.

We know that inheriting a team, whether people you know or strangers, is scary, but for the good of the team, fake it until you feel it. Confidence, that is.

the word

DIANNE NOLAN, COACH

As Women's Basketball Head Coach at Fairfield University in Connecticut, Dianne Nolan has been responsible for recruiting and coaching. As one of the country's best coaches, she has a lot to say about making a team work as one. She shares her tips and experiences with us below.

What do you do when a player is not acting like a member of a team?

I have an open-door policy, and the players know when they are in my office and I close the door, the following discussion is important and confidential. I will close the door and address the issue with the player. I will cite specific examples of behavior that lead me to believe the team is not coming first in the player's mind. I ask the player to explain her actions. After listening, I will outline steps to take so that she can improve her behavior and begin to show her support of team goals.

How do you get the players to work together?

I gather the team together and share an outline of team expectations and goals. I ask for their input. Together we map out a strategy to accomplish the team goal. Daily reminders of the goal are reinforced with signs in the locker room, notes in their lockers, and we have a cheer following practice, yelling out the goal together. Each player fully understands the mission of the team.

How long does it take for a team to gel?

It varies. Every team has its own personality. Each year players mature and graduate and new players join the team. Communication and energy are essential. You must exercise patience and understanding and use the senior members to help the younger players feel comfortable within the team. Each player needs to know their role and how important that role is in accomplishing the team goal. I try to blend the team quickly by sending the team on a scavenger hunt through campus. I divide the team into groups of three. This one-hour exercise has paid enormous dividends in team bonding.

Thoughts about how to integrate a new player in an existing team?
When a player is in their comfort zone, they perform to the best of their ability. I learn as much as I can about the player through non-threatening activities. I need to understand what makes them tick in pressure situations. I set up projects and spend time with each player while she is involved in the project. I access each player's personality and coach her accordingly. I have found you must treat each player fairly but often not the same. They are individuals operating in a team setting.

What do you look for when recruiting players?
Talent, talent, talent. I want players who will help us win ball games, possess the academic credentials to succeed in the classroom, have a strong work ethic, and are good citizens. Playing Division 1 Basketball is challenging, and I look for players who embrace the challenge. They need to be headstrong, have passion, loyalty, and discipline. A good sense of humor is helpful!

Do you have any thoughts about coaching new team members?
Get to know them as quickly as possible. Find our about their family background, their academic history, and their likes and dislikes. The more I really know them, the better I can mesh them with the group. Getting them into a comfort zone is paramount.

What challenges did you face when you took over as coach (regarding acceptance from the players)?
I was a Title IX Baby. The first full-time female coach hired at Fairfield. Every day was a challenge. I had to start from scratch. My first day, I was handed a key to an office with a steel gray desk and nothing in it. I was young and determined. Sometimes ignorance is bliss! I met with the team as soon as possible, outlined my expec-

tations, and away we went. The players were super. Their previous year was not successful and they wanted to be winners. I conveyed nothing is free and we were going to outwork everyone. They bought into the system and worked hard.

How did you earn their respect?
Knowing your craft is so important. If you are going to lead people, you better have a firm grasp of the discipline. Exercising understanding, patience, having energy and self-confidence are important leadership traits. Staying true to your word gains immediate respect. I told the players we were going to work hard and we did. The practices were planned by the minute and were physically and mentally challenging. We worked in the weight room and had rules for campus behavior. Early in my career, after a victory and team celebration at dinner, the players were issued a curfew, since the game was on the road. Later in the evening in the ladies' room, I met two of our star players washing their hands. It was well after curfew. The next game was our Opening Home Tournament, as you can imagine, a very popular event. I suspended the two players and demonstrated to the team that I was true to my word. Respect is earned.

Tips for building an effective team?
Surround yourself with good people. People who are talented, have energy, a good work ethic, integrity, and passion. Do your best when your best is expected.

what do they want from me?

Chances are good that you have at some point been an employee. In fact, unless you own the company, you probably still report to someone. To find out what your people need from you, step back and ask yourself what you need or needed from your higher-ups. Even better, ask yourself what you didn't get and really could have used more of. Your employees need a lot from you.

Here are some of the key things you should be ready, willing, and able to provide:

Clear Vision
You should tell them where the company is going, what their career prospects are, and how you see the team working together.

Support
In every sense of the word, including emotional support (where it pertains to business goals), technical support, logistical support, and staff support to help get their job done.

Respect
For their work, for them as individuals, for their contribution to the organization.

Feedback
We hesitate to say that you are a parental figure, but unfortunately that is the case. At the very least you are an authority figure for your employees, so they are looking to you for feedback on their work. We had an assistant who needed and even asked us for feedback every day. Sure we were busy, but it would make her happy and more productive if we spent a few minutes talking with her.

Answers
They are looking to you to be available for answers on a wide range of subjects. Or at least to help them with finding the solution.

Freedom
One of the best bosses we spoke to, Christine Deussen, president and founder of Deussen Global Communications, Inc., believes

that "Most of all, I think employees need freedom. Freedom to grow and stretch, freedom to make their own mistakes, freedom to try out new ideas. We all continually learn from each other, and if people feel stymied, we will not see their creative best. I am always there as a resource, and of course I will always check up on things until I am comfortable that the work they are putting out is up to our company's standards, but they need to be free to get to the end product in their own way."

shifting employee expectations

There are needs that your employees will expect you to fulfill that you just will not, and should not, be able to. Kathleen Hutchenson, a senior editor at a magazine, had an employee who said she wanted to be Kathleen's friend. She ran a casual and fun team, but that didn't mean that she could befriend the employees. Abigail Disney, founder and president of the Daphne Foundation, shares this: "I learned the hard way that you cannot get too close to people's personal problems when you manage them. Even though you really care about and have compassion for the people you work with, getting too much in the middle of their life's problems can compromise the integrity of the dynamic between you, so it is better to express respect and compassion for them, but to observe and respect their privacy and autonomy at all times."

When you have an employee who makes an impossible request of you, it is a good opportunity to look objectively at what you are projecting to your staff. In your new mode of clear communication, be direct about what you are defining as appropriate. In Kathleen's case she was put in the uncomfortable position of having to tell her employee that while she liked her and enjoyed their working relationship, she had made it a policy not to socialize with employees. If you are not clear with your employees about what is and isn't acceptable to you, you might put yourself in the position of being taken advantage of.

how to tell if you're being taken advantage of

ARE YOUR DEADLINES NOT THE PRIORITY FOR YOUR EMPLOYEES?

As the leader of the team, the deadlines you set for projects need to take precedence over all other tasks. The assumption made by your employees should be that you don't arbitrarily set deadlines. Tell your employees that if you can't trust that they are going to meet deadlines, you can't trust that they are doing their job and that is a huge problem . . . for them.

DO THEY TELL YOU THEY CAN'T DO SOMETHING YOU HAVE DELEGATED?

This is fine, if and only if, once you tell them how to do it or arrange for them to be told, the task gets done. If the answer is "no, it often doesn't get done," then the employee needs to go. They are not performing their job.

DO THEY QUESTION YOUR DIRECTION?

Because we often still have to prove to both sexes that we can do the job as well as men can, it is almost acceptable to question our decisions. Unfortunately, it takes only one disrespecting skeptic on your team to undermine your authority. No one reporting to you should ever question your direction, and if they do so you need to jump all over it.

DO THEY TAKE LONG LUNCHES, CALL IN SICK, LEAVE EARLY?

We have had our share of this in our office, not wanting to be big bitches and call our employees on bad behavior. The problem with letting it go is that it will then happen again and again. By pushing the boundaries that you have set for them, they are testing you to see how much they can get away with. So call it when you see it and don't let anything go.

ARE THEY SPENDING TIME ON PERSONAL PHONE CALLS?

We don't want to say that employees are like children, but sometimes you do feel like the mom when you are standing over them tapping on your watch while they yammer on about their plans for the upcoming weekend. The point is that they will do as much as they can get away with, so you can't let them get away with anything. Your company is paying for their time, and if they are spending it on a personal call, then they are stealing from the company.

WHEN YOU POINT OUT AN ERROR, HOW DO THEY RESPOND?

We had a senior publicist who would cringe when we would point out errors but never, ever took responsibility for them, and an assistant who would give us ten reasons why it happened. Neither of these responses is great. What you want to train your people to do is acknowledge the mistake and take steps, either with you or on their own, to ensure that it won't happen again.

ARE PEOPLE DOING A CARELESS AND/OR CASUAL JOB ON MOST PROJECTS?

If the answer here is yes, then you are being taken advantage of. Especially if you swoop in at the eleventh hour to fine-tune the job before it goes out or is sent upstairs. Unfortunately, this is another trap that women managers seem to fall into more often than their male counterparts. Rather than confront someone with the fact that they did an unacceptable job, women will often want to fix it for them. Do this often enough and your employees will begin counting on the fact that you are not only going to cover their butt but also do their job. The answer is simple: Don't ever accept mediocre work from your people.

ARE THERE POCKETS OF EMPLOYEES WHO SOCIALIZE THROUGHOUT THE DAY?

A little bit of team bonding is a good thing, but too much of it is a waste of company money and can affect the profitability of your group. So break up the huddled masses at the watercooler by calling the ringleader into your office for a quick chat about the latest assignment. If you ignore it (again, women often want to be the good gal), then you are telling your staff that you don't care if they work.

DO YOUR EMPLOYEES NOT STOP TALKING WHEN YOU ENTER A MEETING?

This is a really subtle demonstration of disrespect. When you, the manager of the team, the boss, the head honchette walk into a room, you should be met with quiet anticipation. If, however, you walk into a meeting and the group doesn't wrap up their conversation about the latest episode of *Entourage*, you have a problem. They are showing you that they don't care that much about what you have to say. To take control back from the team, you need to start posturing a little. If you have an assistant, ask him to send an e-mail announcement that you have called a meeting. Make sure that it is outside your weekly meeting so it arrives unexpectedly. Create an agenda and send it around the day before so that the team knows you have set items to discuss. When you walk into the room, stand at the head of the table and make a statement that makes it clear that you are higher up on the ladder and therefore privy to more information about the company than anyone else in the room. Something like "I was at a meeting with the VPs this morning and there are a lot of changes coming down the pike" or "It has been called to my attention that our team is a little behind on sales this month, and this has to turn around starting today." It doesn't have to be a negative statement, but there should be some stakes attached. If they think that you have information that will impact them personally, then you will have their undivided attention.

ARE THEY PUSHING BACK ON ASSIGNMENTS AND SOMEHOW ADDING TO YOUR TO-DO LIST, RATHER THAN MAKING IT SHORTER?

Again, women seem to be suckers for employees-in-need. It takes a will of steel to push back on the sweet project manager asking that something get taken off her plate or the young and eager columnist who needs you to rewrite her copy because you do it so much faster than she does. They work for you, which means you delegate down. If somehow you find that the work is flowing the other way, then it is time for you to start saying no.

gender bending: managing men vs. managing women

Male managers are not the only gender responsible for holding women back in the workplace. A female boss told us that she prefers to manage men because women need too much "hand-holding." Another woman preferred male employees because she felt that they "weren't judging her." Yet another felt more comfortable delegating to men because with women, "I felt I had to ask their permission."

On the flip side, one manager we interviewed preferred women because "I feel it is my mission to encourage women to grow professionally and I feel more invested when I am helping an employee." Anat Baron, an entrepreneur, had some sage advice for us: "In my multiple careers I've always managed both men and women. I treated them the same. I'm a big believer in equality. Everyone gets a fair shake if they perform. I found in general that the stereotypes are true. Men are leery of a female boss (especially in male-dominated industries like hotels and beer) and are constantly testing you to see if you have what it takes. Women, on the other hand, are looking to be 'friends' and are more open with their personal problems. They also expect you to be more understanding. My approach was to deal with everyone fairly. I was clear about expectations, gave people just enough rope, and constantly challenged them to exceed their own expectations of themselves. From the very beginning of my career I was keen to 'develop' employees and was always thrilled to see them move up in their careers. I've always had a zero-tolerance policy for abuse of power, theft, greed, and outright lies. I was always considered a tough boss because I always spoke my mind, but I think most would consider me fair."

Because of how we are socialized, it has become our instinct to treat men and women differently. Be aware of this inadvertently sexist behavior—listening to men over women, asking women to get coffee, assigning the more high-profile assignments to men—and turn things upside down. Even better: Be proactive about turning this dynamic around in the workplace and make an effort to mentor the women on your team. Encourage them to speak up and contribute in meetings. Divide both the glamorous and the dull assignments equitably between men and women. Alternate who makes copies, orders lunch, and cleans up after meetings. As a leader you have an amazing opportunity to do things better than the generation, or even just the boss, that preceded you.

the boss' boss: protecting your staff from the wrath upstairs

Your boss wants you to make her life easier. She wants you to communicate the company's goals to the team and then work with the team to achieve them. Your boss is relying on you to share the appropriate amount of information with your staff. When you are new to the job, she will monitor your recommendations for promotions and punishment. Once you establish trust with your boss and are an effective spokesperson for your team, then those below you will also expect you to be an effective spokesperson for them to the company, to share with them the goals and vision. They also will want you to be their advocate, to win the prestigious assignments and share their accomplishments with your boss. And when things get rough, when deadlines are missed, clients lost, or business slows, they want you to be their protector. So assure them that their jobs are safe, that you will take responsibility for whatever is going on with the higher-ups, and most of all let them know that you appreciate them and their contribution.

girl talk

DEBORAH BLACKWELL

Senior vice president and general manager of SOAPnet, Deborah Blackwell is responsible for all day-to-day operations for this quickly growing twenty-four-hour soap opera channel. A well-respected and well-liked *lady who leads*, Deborah shared with us what she has learned while honing her skills—as a student at Harvard Business School, an agent with William Morris, and in her current position at SOAPnet—as an effective leader.

How would you describe your job as a manager?
I view my job as defining and articulating a vision for SOAPnet, getting the right people into the right jobs, and then empowering and rewarding them.

Define your management style.
"What do you recommend?" is a key phrase for me. When people come into my office with a question, I give them the opportunity to solve the problem themselves. I have found that people will rise to the challenge when I offer them the opportunity. When people come in with suggestions, my goal is that most of the time I take employees' recommendations. That empowers your people to take ownership of their role in the group.

How do you inspire your employees to work harder and work better?
I am interested in people and I try to listen to them. I am a big believer in praising in public and criticizing in private. I make an effort to treat everyone on my team with respect. I say to the team, "We will make mistakes, let's try things and see what happens." I had an old boss who said to me "I am fine if you make mistakes, because if you are afraid to make them, then you won't try anything." And I see the value in that.

What are your challenges when it comes to management and how did you overcome them?
Early on, I had difficulties giving clear direction. Because I hated being bossed around, I would couch things as a suggestion or an idea ("If you have time, you might want to so and so") and finally an assistant said to me, "I don't know what you want me to do." I was overcompensating for my discomfort with my role as an authority in the workplace. I realized that to get the best from people you need to delegate a clear assignment and set a deadline. I also learned that not everyone is ready for total empowerment. Some need more direction and for you to prepare an outline of the steps for a task.

Do you have any advice for first-time managers?

Accept that a work relationship is a different relationship because, for it to run smoothly, there needs to be proper professional distance and that isn't always comfortable in the beginning. When I was promoted early on, I didn't understand why the secretaries treated me differently, were a bit colder and no longer as chummy.

Do you enjoy working for and with women?

I adore working with women, and I have had two female mentors in my career who each taught me to "own" my career and accomplishments. Every time I got a raise and promotion from the first, she would brush aside my gratitude and say, "I am not doing this because I am nice; I am doing this because you are good." The second trusted me to run a business—no small thing. I have worked with and for so many brilliant women that I feel like it is my responsibility to help women come along.

four

don't try this at work

TEN WAYS TO ALIENATE YOUR STAFF

Every girlfriend in the universe has a story about the *Bitch Boss from Hell*. The one who told us we were untalented and would never amount to anything; the one who disappeared for three-hour lunches, but wrote us up if we cut out five minutes early; the one who took credit for our ideas and blamed us for her mistakes.

This unfortunate management style has existed ever since Joan of Arc donned her first suit of armor and led her troops into a losing battle. The most common management missteps are often surprisingly easy to identify and even easier to prevent. By taking a few simple precautions and following (or avoiding) our predecessors' pitfalls, we can all steer clear of these behaviors and get the job done. In other words, you don't need to be a bitch to wield authority and command respect. Just the opposite, in fact.

bad boss behavior 1: letting your insecurities run the office

You have recently been promoted to manage a group of people who were, until this happy news, your professional peers. Looking over your newly acquired staff, you sense resentment, hostility, and skepticism rather than the warm friendly smiles you hoped for. You begin to doubt yourself. What do you have that they don't have? Sheila over there is better at public speaking than you are; how can you possibly tell her what to do? Mark had more sales last quarter than anyone on the team; why would he listen to you?

After your promotion you begin barking orders to overcompensate for the anxiety in the pit of your stomach. You begin to hide in your office. You leave for phantom "very important lunches" to avoid questions from your staff.

Stop! You are letting your insecurities run you and the office.

The tiniest flicker of self-doubt can quickly balloon into a full-blown crisis of confidence. Helen Stephens, travel marketing coordinator for Bacardi, USA, suggests that "when you start finding fault with everything and everyone, look into yourself. More likely than not, you are projecting your insecurities and fears."

If you find yourself doubting your aptitude for your new position, ask yourself if the anxiety actually stems from your lack of professional skills or from floundering self-esteem. If it is the latter, then the best advice (and we know it's easier to give than to follow) is to fake it until you make it. To do this, you project more confidence than you really have. Stand tall, breathe deep, answer and ask questions directly, don't be afraid to say you don't know something, and don't second-guess decisions you have made. Again, posturing comes into play when you want to appear more comfortable in your management role than is really the case. To fake it with your boss, don't let self-doubt creep into your tone when you are presenting ideas, sales figures, or campaign ideas. Your comfort level will increase the longer you are in your position and as soon as you sail through a tricky project.

If you determine that you do, in fact, lack certain skills, then tackle the deficiencies head-on: Take a class, read a manual, and/or get some training (there are weekend seminars on almost everything these days, from management to marketing) so that you will no longer feel like a dope when you are talking to your staff about their areas of expertise. Keep all of this training to yourself. The last thing you want is for your staff to make your remedial training the subject of watercooler gossip. One woman we interviewed wrote us to say that if you are insecure, "keep it #$%@ to yourself! You are a leader, but that doesn't come with the title. You have to earn the respect of your staff, and if you behave like a child they will not respect you."

Your insecurity can also impair the growth of your team. You might start avoiding tough assignments because you don't feel capable of leading your people through them. Or alienating your staff with unintentional hostility. When we asked Liza, a former editor of a women's magazine, about this bad boss behavior, she laughed and told us, "Okay. I did this. Totally. With the woman who had been hired the same week as me. It was extraordinary how she managed to massage every insecurity of mine, especially considering how underwhelmed I was by her skills and performance. I was always looking for her approval—I don't know why. Even worse, because we were in this weird position where technically she reported to me but we were hired the same week and never got a chance to establish the pecking order, I tried to be her friend to overcompensate for my discomfort. I mean, I probably would've tried to be her friend anyway, but the situation was, like, the perfect storm that brought my managerial foibles to the surface."

bad boss behavior 2: not leading by example

This is the one where the standards you set for yourself are radically different from the standards you have for your employees. Admitting this behavior takes brutal self-honesty. Do you often leave early, but expect your staff to stay late? Do you take long lunches, personal calls, and spend a chunk of the Monday morning meeting talking about your weekend, but reprimand your employees if they do the same? We had a boss who unloaded all of her work on her underlings, took off every summer Friday regardless of how busy it was, and worst of all, "asked" her assistants to baby-sit her kids during their personal time.

None of that is cool. Being the boss doesn't mean that you're now entitled to lead a cushy life. On the contrary, you should be the hardest worker in the office. If, for example, your staff sees that you are the first to arrive, last to leave, and that you rarely go out for lunch, then it's tough for them to find excuses not to work hard themselves. To gain the respect of those who work for you, it's essential that you lead by example, inspiring your staff to mimic your very own professional behavior. Act as you would like your best employee to act. Jump in to help, don't talk about others behind their backs, be honest, work hard, respect others, and most of all . . . enjoy the job.

Remember that you are the epicenter of the team; your behavior, attitude, style, manner, sense of self, and ambition influence everyone around you. So elevate the expectations you have for yourself and with your capable and enthusiastic attitude inspire those who report to you.

good witch or big bitch?

THE BOSS FRIEND

Here's a story from our friend Mindy Pine:

With one boss, I fell into the trap—I thought we were friends. For three years, I loved working for her—and talking about Sex and the City *on Monday mornings, and shoes and makeup and shopping and all that kind of chat you do with a girlfriend over brunch. I worked for her when I met my husband, and she loved hearing all about our courtship. When we became engaged, my boss was one of the first people I wanted to call.*

Cut to—major changes at work, new structures, and suddenly I'm dropped. I'm out of the loop. Yes, I still have my job, but no chat time, no girlfriend time. She's too busy making friends with the new people who have joined our division. While at a sales conference, she grabbed a few quiet minutes with me to catch up. She asked how my husband was doing, how his job was (I had shared many times with her how stressful it was). I said he was holding tough.

A month later, I was told that my position was being eliminated, and that there wasn't a place for me in the new organization. I then knew why she had been asking about my husband's job. This was almost the most upsetting thing to me—I had looked to her as a role model, someone who made a big salary in a male-dominated industry, an example of a woman making it in this business. Now my role model was making sure that my husband could take (financial) care of me. Worse than that, because of her interest in my personal life, I had thought we were friends.

Big Bitch. Gone are the days when you can be everyone's gal pal. No more scooting off to the lunchroom to spend an hour chatting about the latest episode of *Desperate Housewives*. When asked what was the biggest mistake they made as first-time managers, almost all of the women we interviewed replied "befriending our employees." You are not there to be anyone's friend. You are in the leadership role to provide the tools and environment that your team needs to accomplish their goals. And when you have blurred the lines of what should be a strictly professional relationship and then pull out the rug from under your employee when things get tough, you are a Big Bitch.

bad boss behavior 3: gender discrimination: don't forget to take care of your own

According to many women we interviewed, it is common for male bosses to be more comfortable around those of their own gender. Helen Stephens wrote us to say, "This familiarity is an instant 'bond' with the known gender and unless the manager makes a concerted effort to not play favorites based on sex, this behavior is palpable and lethal in promoting the team atmosphere so needed in a department/office environment." By the same token, there are many female bosses who, because they have been socially conditioned to defer to men, will favor their male employees. So women in the workplace can often feel neglected by their male managers and overlooked by their female managers. Now that you are the chick-in-charge, it is your opportunity to run things differently. Be aware that you may be judging your female employees unfairly, and based on male professional behavior. Teach your female employees to speak up for themselves. Give them opportunities to shine by soliciting their input and ideas in public meetings.

bad boss behavior 4: leave them alone: why micromanaging blows!

If you are jumping in on every little decision, project phase, and trip to the bank, then you are wasting both your time and your employees' time. One woman we spoke to said she began to "just dial it in" when she realized her boss wouldn't let her do anything on her own. If you are micromanaging, then you are not maximizing *their* potential. When you treat your staff like children, guess what happens? They start acting like children, unable to make decisions without your input, and clamoring for your attention on projects big and small. But the biggest reason it blows? It means you are setting a poor managerial style, causing your staff to devolve rather than evolve and essentially shooting yourself in the foot. Many of the women we spoke to were guilty of micromanaging. Samantha Reese, the owner of a small business, shares this insight. "Sure I try not to micromanage, but I have been juggling two kids, a husband, ten employees, a dog, two houses, and a car for the past fifteen years. To keep all the balls in the air I have to be pretty on top of everything and it isn't so easy to let go."

Juli Tolleson, an account director at US Concepts, shares this story about the effects of micromanaging on your staff. "I had an assistant account executive who was sometimes very slow to turn around important assignments. This made me panic at times, and I began to send her several e-mails requesting updates every time she had a project. This didn't go over well with her, and she began to either ignore my e-mails or give snappy responses. I was upset by the fact that she didn't seem to respect me very much, but realized that she was generally nice and talented, and that I should talk with her to find out what I was doing wrong and figure out a way to make it work. She appreciated my going to her, explained that she felt like I was micromanaging her and that it interfered with her work and made her less motivated to do the projects. I explained that I understood why that would be upsetting, but that she'd missed a few deadlines, so I felt nervous each time I gave her a time-sensitive project. I asked her what she suggested we do to fulfill both of our needs. She suggested a daily update e-mail, which was great. Moving forward, I stopped bugging her with update requests, and she made her deadlines. It worked because instead of me telling her what to do, I gave her the objective and asked her for the best solution. That made her feel empowered and respected, and eager to do good work. And I got what I needed, too."

ARE YOU TOO CONTROLLING?

There is a fine line between doing your job of managing and micromanaging. Micromanaging is formally defined as *paying extreme attention to the small details.* In our daily work life it means having a manager over your shoulder at all times questioning your decisions, directing you on every aspect of an assignment, giving you zero autonomy, and not letting you make your mark. To make sure you are not one of these annoying and ineffective managers, take this quick quiz.

1. Do you edit *everything* (even incidental correspondence to nonessential third parties)?
2. Do you check up on people several times a day while they are busy working on something you have assigned?
3. Do you insist on attending *every* meeting?
4. Do you find yourself questioning your employees' decisions (both big and small)?
5. Do you step in when your reports are trying to delegate to their staff?
6. Do you delegate only the inconsequential assignments?

7. Do you find yourself e-mailing your employees throughout the day with additional tasks, questions, instructions, requests for updates, etc., rather than consolidating these requests into global policies?

If you answered yes to more than a few of those questions, you are a control freak. Surprised? We didn't think so. To have gotten to this phase in your career, you have had to be on top of everything. And clearly you were good at it, because you have now been entrusted with managing others. But your job has changed, and being a control freak about your own projects and career is very different from how you now need to guide others. You need to teach, explain, direct, and mentor your reports, not do their work for them. This is going to be a rocky transition as you begin to let go of the little stuff, so take it slow. Reduce the amount of times you check in with people by one, skip one or two meetings a week, let your reports delegate to their staff without input from you, and request a weekly status e-mail from your employees rather than a daily one.

bad boss behavior 5: unreasonable expectations and criticisms

As a junior sales executive (only a mini step up from an assistant), Lisa Blake had an employer who expected her to come to the table with ideas, input, and problem solving that come only with years' worth of experience. For her, only a few months into a profession, this seemed insane. The employer's unreasonable expectations led to unreasonable criticisms, as she was constantly berated and put down for not having more to offer. Eleven months into this job, Lisa had to quit. Lisa ended up just fine; in fact, within four years she had founded her own business. Just imagine how much her employer might have gotten from her over the years. As for reasonable criticisms, Trae Bodge, cofounder and creative director of Three Custom Color Specialists, says not to be afraid of criticizing or expecting things from our staff, pointing out that "it's hard, especially when you work closely with someone, to comment on their work and how it could improve. But remember, you are doing something good for them as well as for the workplace, so it should (when done fairly) only strengthen your relationship."

When assigning tasks, be realistic about the time frame you are setting for completion. It will help everyone if as the manager you are keeping track of what is on your employees' plates. Your people-pleasing staff members won't tell you when they are doing too much and will just take on more until they are buried. As manager, you need to be aware of their to-do list at all times. We had a situation with an employee who just kept taking on additional client work at team meetings. She would pipe up, hand held high, and say "I would love to work on that" whenever we introduced a new project. When she began missing deadlines and the quality of her work started going downhill fast, we were really frustrated. We felt like she wasn't meeting our expectations until we took stock of her to-do list and realized we were being completely unrealistic.

When setting your expectations for your employees, you also need to keep in mind their strengths and weaknesses. If you have an employee who is a great writer but not very fast, then don't assign him a project that has a short deadline. If you have someone who is a creative thinker but new to the business, then know that he won't be the one coming up with the home-run ideas at a brainstorm but will help move the thinking forward.

And lastly, be clear with the staff about what you consider to be a good job when you are assigning projects. The lazy boss is one who delegates a task with little direction and without a definition of success, then explodes when her expectations are not met. If you want to see thirty units sold by next Thursday, then tell your staff that is what you mean when you say "increase sales this week." If you want a completed proposal by Sunday, then say that rather than "get it done quickly." If you define the expectations for your team and they are not met, then and only then can you reasonably criticize.

the word

TIPS FROM DR. DORRI JACOBS, MEDIATOR

Dr. Dorri Jacobs, a NYC work issues coach, mediator, and internationally published author, gives us some advice about conflict resolution, firing, and suggestions for handling some of the stickier management situations.

Do you have thoughts for how we can become better managers?
Trust employee competence. Rather than criticize, allow individuals to explain where they could do better and what resources they lack (information, staff, equipment, time). Give praise often.

As a manager you are often put in the position of mediating. What is the goal behind mediating in the workplace?
Mediation empowers people to resolve their problems by working together. The parties involved have an opportunity to speak, to listen to each other, to create and discuss possible solutions that will satisfy both of them.

Tips for firing someone with dignity?
Be honest. Be humane. Be kind. Give the person some notice, rather than expect him or her to leave the same day. If it is your decision, explain why she/he is being let go. If it is part of a major downsizing, and not your decision, say so. If it is a performance issue, make sure the employee knew about the problem and had been given an opportunity to improve. Give the employee a good

reference letter, and say potential employers can contact you as well.

Tips for conflict resolution?
Make sure there is enough time for all involved to express their needs and feelings, to really hear each other. No quick fixes: Do not jump at the first "solution" without verifying each of their reactions. Be willing to go further if need be, so they can come up with an answer that truly pleases each of them. Get training so you are comfortable with conflict and with people talking on an emotional level.

bad boss behavior 6: treating your assistant as your husband, nanny, valet, housekeeper, or best friend

To avoid treating your assistant as anything other than an assistant, create a job description (containing only work-related tasks) before you interview a candidate, and then once she is hired, stick to it. Sounds easy, right? Not so much, especially on those days when you are trapped in meetings all day and can't find fifteen minutes to run to the bank or you are packing up for a sales conference and need to pick up dry cleaning. If you don't want to be cast as an entitled and unprofessional boss from hell, please, please, please don't go off the list and ask your eager assistant to get your shoes resoled, pick up nail polish for you, deposit your paycheck, buy a birthday card for your mom, or anything else that smacks of the personal. Helen Stephens reminds us that your assistant "will feel demeaned and eventually resentful of your assumption that she will also take care of you personally." In most cases your assistant is being paid to assist you with your *job* only—so go ahead and ask her to book your travel for a business trip, but don't tell her to research your vacation to Morocco.

As far as being a best friend, this is a distinctly female trap. Not enough of us have the right balance between being friendly but professional and being a friend. You can't be a friend to your employee, even though you may adore her. Your loyalty has to be to the company you work for, and you complicate things for both of you when you make a professional relationship personal.

A note about keeping things businesslike in the office: Don't go overboard. Believe it or not, it is possible to be *too* professional with your staff. We had a boss who didn't share a single bit of personal information with us. After two years of working for her we didn't know where she lived, if she was married, or even what she did before she arrived at the job. She didn't even have a personal photo on her desk or on her bookshelf. We knew that she was trying to maintain the "proper" distance, but it left her staff feeling unengaged. It was so extreme that when she left for a new job there was barely a murmur among the staff and we quickly embraced her replacement. You want your team to support you, and even care about you enough to work hard for you. To make that happen, they should like you, at least a little. We know it sounds counterintuitive, but by sharing a few key personal tidbits with your staff you become a living, breathing human being for them, not just an authority figure, and it is easier to work hard for a Jessica than a Boss. Do tell them where you went to college, how you found yourself in this career, about your first job experience, what you love about the profession, and even your favorite place to vacation. Don't tell them about the first time you got drunk, anything about your romantic life, conflicts that you may be having with others at the company, your long-term vision for your career, or any topic you cover in therapy. If you strike the perfect balance between too much information and not enough, your staff will both like you and respect you.

EIGHT HABITS TO PASS ON

As a manager you have a captive audience. You can set the bar for how your people act and perform as members of your team. You also have the young and eagers looking to you for how to behave professionally, so teach them well. To get the best from everyone on a day-to-day basis, demonstrate great work habits.

Be Clean

Don't have paperwork stacked on your desk, artwork askew, extra shoes piled in the corner, half-full coffee mugs and dying plants in your office. If you maintain a clean, professional office space, chances are good they will, too.

Q&As

When your team approaches you with a question, answer it right away. If you don't know the answer, then say you don't know the answer but will find out. It will teach your employees not to make up answers because they are too ashamed to admit they don't know something. Similarly, you can inspire your team to jump in on problems the right way by demonstrating that when you are faced with one, you find out all of the details before offering an off-the-cuff solution.

To-dos

Teach your team to spend a few minutes at the end of each day to jot down the to-do list for the upcoming day. It is an efficient way to use those last twenty useless minutes of the day.

E-mail Is Not Snail Mail

When your team sends you e-mails, answer them right away. You don't want to make them wait for answers they need to proceed with their work, and you also don't want to imply that it's okay to procrastinate.

Be On Time

Show up for everything on time. If you are late to meetings, appointments, reviews, or anything else, you are demonstrating that you are fine with tardiness. Since you are teaching them to be ideal employees, teach them to be on time.

Looking Professional

Again, even if you believe that you get more creative thinking done in your favorite pair of jeans, don't wear them to the office. You want to inspire your employees to dress professionally.

Don't Drink

If you are taking your staff out to lunch, don't order that glass of wine. If you are out with a client and a member of your team, pass on the cocktail. If you keep it to sparkling water, soda, or juice when you are on the clock, then your people will too, but if you make it okay to drink during office hours, you are setting a dangerous precedent. Ask yourself if you are comfortable with your employees drinking while out to lunch with clients?

Always Be Prepared

When presenting to your team or your client, make sure you are prepared. Not only does it help you with your own level of confidence, but it encourages your staff to hone their own knowledge before jumping into a meeting or presentation.

bad boss behavior 7: thinking your employees have esp

Do you want your employees scurrying around you anxiously because they are trying to figure out exactly what it is you want them to do and how you want them to do it? We hope the answer is "of course not!" That's what happens when there is an expectation of ESP. While someone who has worked with you for a while might have developed instincts regarding your preferences, that is almost never the case with new folks. Make it easier on everyone by reviewing directions and expectations clearly and concisely. Remember that too many people fill in lack of information with negative assumptions (she doesn't like me, she is avoiding me, I am going to be fired, I did something wrong), so give your employees a break and tell them exactly what you want.

bad boss behavior 8: taking credit without giving it

It is pretty bad to take credit for other people's work and worse when you never give nods for jobs well done. Before you skip this paragraph because you think that you would never do this, consider this scenario: Your VP has assigned you a report to write and you pull in your team to help you with the project. Two weeks after handing it in, the VP has finally had a chance to review it and calls you into the office to say "great job!" The rest of the day gets nutty and you don't mention the feedback to the team. Are you taking credit without giving it? Yes. Is it intentional? Maybe not. Would your boss have wanted you to praise your team in that moment? Maybe, maybe not. Maybe she assumes that having a crackerjack group is part of your job. Either way, a good manager would pull together everyone who contributed to the report moments after leaving the VP's office to congratulate and praise them, or at least sends the team an e-mail. They made you look good and for that they deserve credit and thanks. If one too many instances go by where you don't take the time to acknowledge their contribution, you will be stuck with a staff that lacks ambition, interest, and engagement.

bad boss behavior 9: crying, screaming, and losing your temper

Almost everyone we interviewed for this book had a bad boss story that featured a woman who was a screamer or crier. This is unfortunate because we get a bad rap in the workplace for being overemotional anyway, and it takes only a few criers out there in corporate America to perpetuate the stereotype. If you scream only occasionally and cry only once in a blue moon, that is still way, way too much. If you have gotten to the point of exhibiting any extreme emotion in the office, you have failed somewhere along the line and need to rein it in. If you are a yeller, then try the ten-second method. When something angers you, before responding or tackling the issue, take a breath that lasts five seconds going in and five seconds going out. By the time you are taking the second breath, you should be calm enough to discuss something without yelling. If you are a crier, there are so many reasons to turn this behavior around. First and foremost, people lose respect for bosses who cry. Imagine you are in your boss's office; she has just received the news that the company has lost an account and has started crying in front of you. Beyond awkward, this behavior is downright strange. As adults, crying is just not the thing to do. It doesn't inspire confidence or respect. It does inspire compassion, sympathy, and maybe a little pity. But do you want to be pitied by your assistant? The worst aspect of this behavior: You are giving off the vibe that it is okay to be highly emotional in the workplace when it isn't.

bad boss behavior 10: being a jealous julie

Jealousy is an insidious emotion that rears its ugly head in the most inappropriate ways. Sometimes you are faced with managing someone who is a brilliant and creative thinker or even someone who has more potential than you do (only if you are really honest with yourself would you ever admit this). If you don't know yourself very well and find yourself treating this blessed employee worse than everyone else, jealousy could be at work. We spoke to Anat Baron, a former Hollywood producer and current entrepreneur, who had a "jealous Julie" in her life. "When I had a producing deal, I worked with (not for) a VP of Development who was in my hair all the time. She had to know who I was talking to, eating lunch with, etc. When it came time to renew my deal, I was in Europe attending a friend's wedding. She was so petty and jealous that she didn't get invited (the couple were another producer and an agent) that she ensured that my checks stopped coming and that I found out about it while I was away. I came back and packed up my stuff. Life is too short to be around that type of energy." If you feel resentment toward an employee, keep in mind that it is just your competitive nature gone awry and remind yourself that if your employee succeeds, then you succeed.

girl talk

LOUISE JORDAN, PR EXECUTIVE

To offer us the other point of view, we spoke to Louise Jordan, an account executive at Deussen Global Communications, about her thoughts on being managed.

Did you notice any management characteristics that were common among your female bosses?

They can be too emotional. Oftentimes, I have had female bosses who, if they are having a bad day, somehow that makes it okay to take it out on me. Also, in many cases I think I was threatening to them. Instead of wanting to take a more mentor role and be happy to help me grow, it was almost like they wanted to hold me back. In the worst cases, it was straight-out jealousy.

Did many of your female bosses try and befriend you rather than keep it professional?

Yes, I had this one boss who always wanted me to go out with her. When I couldn't go or I had something else to do, it was very uncomfortable because I felt like I was hurting her feelings, and she would act a little pissed off at me during the workday. It was like being stuck between a rock and a hard place.

That being said, I do think that you can have a friendship with your boss; it doesn't have to be all business all the time. I mean, we are all human.

But there just has to be an understanding that there is a boss-employee boundary that you can't cross and that as the boss you can't abuse your power over your employee.

How do you like to be managed?

I like a boss to give me a project or a task, explain in detail what he wants (but allow flexibility if I have ideas or thoughts), and then let me run with it. Then we meet back to discuss how it is going, any changes that need to be made, etc. This way I feel like we are connected, but I am not being micromanaged.

Also, it is really important to give positive feedback. All people want to feel like they are doing a good job. Of course, they have to be doing a good job to get positive feedback. I had a boss who never told me I was doing anything right. It was always what I was doing wrong, and that really frustrated me to no end, and made me not want to do well. It is really discouraging if you feel like nothing you do is good enough.

What did you learn from previous managers?

Having had challenging managers, I actually think I am going to be a good one. I think I am much more patient than I used to be because I had one boss who was so moody and hard to work with that I learned to just relax, be calm, and let her bad mood blow over. In the past, I would have gotten really upset and let it get to me. Now I have learned that getting emotional in the workplace is never a good idea. It is better to walk away and calm down. That being said, I also learned to speak up for myself. I mean just because you have to work for someone, doesn't mean they can treat you any way they want.

Anything else you want to share?

One last point: In a business world where men still make more than women do for the same jobs, and 95 percent of all CEO and top positions are held by men, I think that women should support each other and help each other, instead of feeling threatened by another woman. I know this has been said time and time again, for many things, but it is true. In a way, it has been very good for me to be so poorly managed by a couple of women bosses, because I know that I will never do that when I'm the boss.

communicate. motivate. celebrate.

Now that you have a solid team in place, how do you keep them motivated and happy? In all the books we've read, in all the interviews we've done, and in all the research we've seen, the advice is the same: Communicate. Communicate in a positive way. Share good news. Criticize privately, praise publicly. Have an open-door policy. Don't talk, listen. There's no "I" in team. Create We. It all sounds great, but how do you actually do it?

A human resources director of a four-hundred-person engineering firm with offices in New York, New Jersey, Pennsylvania, and Florida told us that in her exit interviews with more than fifty employees in the last six months, they all gave the same reason for leaving: "Not enough communication from senior management."

Not enough communication from management? If you asked us a couple of years ago for the main reason why people leave jobs, we would have undoubtedly said because they want to make more money. But what we're hearing over and over is that communication is key. Employees want to know what's expected of them. Libby Sartain, Chief People Yahoo! (head of human resources of Yahoo!), says that in her thirty-year career, she's noticed that most people come to work every day wanting to give their best and add value. And if they do what's expected of them, they want to know they can expect in return.

Sure, part of the return is compensation. But there is so much more. Remember, people *want* to do a good job. So how do you help them do a good job? And keep them motivated and inspired when they come to work each day? How do you give your team what they need to succeed? This chapter looks at what good managers can do to keep their employees happy.

it's a two-way street

Wow. There are a lot of unhappy people in the workplace. Searching around the Internet, we found a number of sites where people complain about their bosses, including: www.iworkwithfools.com, www.oddtodd.com, www.revengelady.com as well as sections on www.ivillage.com and www.ivillage.co.uk where people can anonymously post complaints about their bosses and coworkers. There's even a blog-hosting community at www.fthisjob.com that says: "Welcome to fthisjob.com, the 'I hate my job' blogging community. Here at fthisjob.com, we believe that job blogging helps you better deal with those asshole customers, stupid boss decisions and other daily crap you get at work everyday."

"Other daily crap you get at work everyday"? That is some terrible attitude. Sure we've all had crappy jobs, but can you honestly say that all of the time it was because your managers were terrible? Once in a while can you admit that your skills weren't matched up with the position? We can.

Early in our careers, both of us worked at the same high-energy public relations company. It was our first experience at an actual agency, and boy was it eye-opening. We were impressed by the people who we worked with—they were smart, highly motivated, and results oriented. From the minute you entered the door, you knew you had to perform or move on. There was no real training, yet everybody seemed to excel. It was exciting and scary at the same time. Each day we felt we were one mistake away from losing our jobs. We learned as much as we could, did as well as we could, and got the heck out of there in a year. Somehow, though, that agency made a lasting impression on us. We now greatly admire the founder of the agency and even seek out his advice for our business. We don't want to run our shop in the same manner, yet we marvel at the caliber of people he consistently hired and the quality of work he was able to get out of them. It wasn't always pleasant, but it was certainly productive. And if we were to be really honest, we would admit that we didn't do our best work there and it wasn't management's fault. Yet, when you read these complaint-filled Web sites, you never see anyone take responsibility for their part. They are all victims of bad management and bad communication.

When faced with bad management, we offer the same advice that your therapist will give you when you're in a bad relationship: Examine yourself. Look honestly at your performance and your own communication skills and see if you can make any changes to your approach so you will get a better result. Remember, there are two sides to every story.

the word

Judith calls herself an organizational anthropologist and coach. She brings new insights to leaders by creating We-centric workplaces that support the growth and development of people, partnerships, and a thriving business. As a master coach, facilitator, and organizational designer, she works with clients to raise the bar and achieve the next level of success through a process she calls the "journey." This process catalyzes new ways of thinking and new types of courageous vital conversations, and enables leaders to redefine challenges, rethink strategies, reinvent new products and services, build strong partnerships with customers, leverage mergers and acquisitions, and create new business models that drive profitability and growth—with a direct line of sight to the customer.

Her clients span a wide variety of industries and are organizations seeking to sustain a leadership position by revitalizing their strategic business focus to become more competitive, profitable, and higher performing. These include clients such as Siemens, Pfizer, Coach, Lipton, VeriSign, Thomson, Novartis, Verizon, Citibank, Donna Karan International, Exide Technologies, and Clairol.

Judith shares her thoughts on creating a positive environment through healthy, We-centric conversations:

You have to remember that there's a human being on the other end of a conversation. I encourage my clients to listen without judgment, and every time I remind them that the premier skill set for an effective leader is to create space for other people, not take it away. You should know that words will either cause us to bond and trust more fully and think of others as friends and colleagues, or they will cause us to break rapport and think of others as enemies.

Through my years of consulting, I've noticed that as you grow up into a business, you're driven from position of power to position of power, from one box to another. If you're driven only by positional power, then you start to assume the behaviors that destroy companies. In my book I list the main behaviors that cause companies and executives to fail:

- Lack of shared focus, shared purpose, and/or shared vision
- Lack of enterprise-wide communication
- Lack of organizational ambition and a strategic approach for getting there
- Lack of respect for others within the organization
- Failure to tap resources and inner talent, creativity, and responsibility
- Failure to break down walls ("silos") between divisions
- Lack of team cohesion and failure to develop team agreements, rules of engagement, and decision-making processes
- Failure to focus outside and see the customer
- Lack of hope and spirit; a punishing environment

To allow for executives and companies to succeed, they must have the ability to:

- Have healthy conversations that build a sense of common purpose and assert a strong leadership voice and laser-sharp focus on the work that needs to be done
- Clarify organizational ambition and create a strategic focus that encourages employees to step out of their comfort zones and take action in the face of ambiguity
- Leave behind the toxic, emotional baggage of the past and tap into new resources and underused talents by encouraging creativity and responsibility
- Exchange knowledge and wisdom between groups
- Have vital conversations that challenge all parties in creative ways

- *Create and live by team agreements, rules of engagement, and a clear decision-making process*
- *Redefine challenging circumstances in creative ways, to tell new stories with an external focus that connect the needs of customers, exploit and shape future trends, and reposition business for category leadership*
- *Focus on the positives, celebrate success, grow from failure, and build hope and spirit into the organizational DNA—to repeatedly create and achieve critical milestones of success and, most importantly,*
- *Be able to find one's voice and be fearless in creating a "We-centric organization" that fosters an attitude of "we are in this together"*

the m-word: gotta give good meetings

We're not big fans of meetings. We're a small company in an open-plan office where communication just happens. We listen to one an-others' conversations, glean what we need to know, keep our heads down, and get the work done—in our case generating media results for our clients. Or so we thought. We found that our "eavesdrop your way to success" method of communication wasn't happening. Goals weren't being met. Staff didn't know what was expected of them or what their priorities were. Where had we gone wrong? We were try-ing to create a culture where people acted as we did—they knew what they had to do and did it. How could we so quickly forget our early career experience?

We had to find a way to give the team what they needed. We were surprised when the answer presented itself in a place where we would have never considered looking—a meeting. We had a horrible staff meeting one morning when we found out that the placements (articles written about our clients) we needed were not happening. We had to set the goals in very specific terms for one of our publicists. We told her exactly what we needed and when it was due. We both felt terrible. If that had happened to either of us in a meeting, we would have died of humiliation. Yet what we found was an amazing transformation. Without the weight of figuring out her goals and deadlines, our publicist was free to execute. And she executed brilliantly. She's an excellent publicist, just not a good time manager. So we have to help her structure her time. Not a big deal, if it helps her excel at her job. Remember, if she excels, we excel.

focus on the future: career development planning

The hardest thing for a business to recover from is the loss of an employee. Even a mediocre one has been trained and can be coached to the next level. It's important to think as much about your individual employee's future within your organization as it is to think about meeting your sales goal. Creating career development plans is a great way to get you and your employees on the same page about their future.

A career development plan lays out a list of long- and short-term goals for each employee, both for the job they are in and the one they are working toward. For example, a salesperson will not only have their sales goals listed, they will have benchmarks they are required to reach before they will be promoted to sales manager.

Also, outline a planned sequence of formal and informal experiences to assist the employee in achieving her goals. It's important to discuss the employee's personal hopes and dreams as well. Libby Sartain, Chief People Yahoo!, had just finished a career development plan with one of her employees before we interviewed her. She explained that the personal goals often figure prominently into the plans. This employee had young children at home and he wanted to make sure that he wouldn't be relocated or asked to travel for long periods at a time. He made it clear that his future in the company was linked to remaining in the Bay Area. If you are working on a plan with an employee, he should have a tremendous say in his future because you want to retain the best people on your team.

The career development goals should be linked to the person's potential. Ultimately, the purpose of a career development plan is to help the employee in achieving his goals. In doing so, an organization also increases the likelihood of retaining him, because the manager has helped the worker consider how to achieve career goals within the organization, rather than by leaving it.

Another benefit of the career development plan is to help employees set realistic expectations for their movement up the ranks. The plan should suggest time frames for certain milestones like promotions and identify specific areas that need to develop before the next milestone. The plans aren't commitments, but rather a road map for the future. Give an explanation of your half of the bargain: "If you do this, this, and this, then you should expect that, that, and that."

Here are the steps for career development planning:

- Meet with your employee to identify his long-term career interests. Specifically, ask him to outline his goals for the short term (one year) and long term (two to five years). Also ask him about his current job: Is he interested in receiving any special assignments, participating in any training courses, acquiring any new skills, or contributing in new ways to the department?
- Don't forget to ask about family and community goals. Is he able or interested in relocating?
- After the meeting, sit down with your management and figure out if you can deliver on the employee's desired goals. If you can't, you need to try to figure out why and propose an alternate solution.

- Prepare the plan and set another meeting to review it together. Give him a copy and put one in his personnel file. Make sure you track his progress throughout the year and discuss it during the performance review. If he is way ahead, adapt the plan accordingly. If he is way behind, try to get him back on track or adapt the plan accordingly.

good witch or big bitch?

SOME BITCHES ARE CRAZY
A scary story from our friend Aleta Jones:

I was hired as managing editor of a bridal Web site—which was then an umbrella site for several different magazines (an unhappy arrangement, to say the least)—on the last day of my honeymoon. The site was about to go through a major upgrade of its operating system, which had been custom designed according to the specifications of my boss, Justine. In fact, the notion to make the bridal Web site the umbrella for too many magazines was Justine's idea, one I imagine she was able to execute because, as I would soon learn, she screamed so much and so hysterically that people must've said yes just to get her out of their offices. The week I was hired, Justine had also hired an editorial assistant who would function as her assistant as well. This was the second week of November. On Thursday of my first week, Justine announced she was resigning and wouldn't be back after Thanksgiving. Her promise was that in the two and a half weeks that remained, she'd make herself available to train us. I was told that I would take over the editing of the site without a raise, her office, or her assistant.

The next two weeks were like a bad dream that just kept getting worse. A typical incident: I go to Justine's office with a question about some aspect of the functionality of the new system.

The door is open, I knock and step in. Justine is on the ground on her hands and knees. I say, "Justine?" She screams "Not now! I'm doing something really important!" Turns out, she was looking for a bead that fell off her necklace. Now, I respect the role of jewelry in one's life as much as anyone—but really. This was her idea of being available and about the extent of the knowledge transfer I got from her about the new system. I'm still amazed by her profound lack of responsibility for the Web site, the project, and her hires that she demonstrated in that period. What was even worse, though, than her behavior toward the staff, was the extent to which she had alienated nearly every department she worked with—especially Information Technology. Not only was I thrust into a role that I was unprepared for, but I had to spend six months rebuilding bridges that she had burned to a crisp. The icing on the cake? She tried to recruit me for the start-up she was leaving for.

Sometimes, managers are just crazy. If you're lucky, they will quit or get fired. If they don't leave, then find another job, or another manager.

we all win!: goal-setting to bring your team together

Individual goals. Team goals. Departmental goals. Corporate goals. At every level and every step of the way you need goals to succeed. Most of the self-help books on the market will tell you that the first step to achieving your goal is to say it out loud. And then write it down. Dr. Phil calls it, "Name It to Claim It."

Daisy Martinez hosts a PBS cooking show and is one of our clients. She was also Dr. Phil's first "Name It to Claim It" girl on the *Oprah Winfrey* show in 1999. She submitted her story to *Oprah's* Web site and since then has achieved more than she ever imagined.

For as long as she could remember, Daisy wanted to be a professional cook. She had grown up cooking Latino food at her *abuela*'s side. She put aside her dreams to raise her family (she's the mother of four) and support her husband through medical school and his residency. For her fortieth birthday, her husband gave her a surprise gift—enrollment in the French Culinary Institute in New York City—and the opportunity to make her dreams come true. She began cooking professionally and was discovered while she worked as a prep cook on another cooking show. In spring 2005, *Daisy Cooks!* first aired on PBS, and in the fall of 2005, Daisy published her first cookbook of the same name. Her current goal is to go back on the *Oprah Winfrey Show* and actually cook for Oprah.

Individually and as an organization, setting goals gives you long-term vision and short-term motivation. It focuses you on the acquisition of knowledge and helps you to identify and organize your resources so you can better achieve your goals.

Goal-setting helps you:
- Decide what's important
- Separate the relevant from the irrelevant
- Motivate to achieve your goals
- Improve your performance
- Improve your self-confidence by keeping track of your successes

A good goal statement needs to be specific. It needs to be measurable, action-oriented, realistic, and tangible. Big goals (I want to write a book) should be broken down into smaller goals (Come up with an idea. Create an outline. Research. Write a proposal. Find an agent, etc.) and then written down. Make a commitment to accomplishing them and then remind yourself to stay on track by setting deadlines. Don't forget to review and reassess your goals on a regular schedule.

Goal-setting for organizations is as important as it is for individuals. Your team needs to know what they are trying to achieve and how they fit into the bigger picture. When we were in book publishing, we had a manager who used to say, "Don't think like a publicist. Think like a publisher," meaning don't focus on generating placements, focus on generating placements and putting out messages that will sell books. The goal wasn't to generate placements, but to sell books.

put your money where your mouth is: dollars and sense

Second to good communication is good money. And we would argue that even if an employee worked in a communication utopia, if another company with horrible communication offered to double her salary for the same position, she'd be out the door in a heartbeat. What's really fair? According to www.dol.gov: "The department of labor enforces the Fair Labor Standards Act (FLSA), which sets basic minimum wage and overtime pay standards. These standards are enforced by the Department's Wage and Hour Division, a program of the Employment Standards Administration.

"Workers who are covered by the FLSA are entitled to a minimum wage of not less than $5.15 an hour (in 2005). Overtime pay at a rate of not less than one and one-half times their regular rate of pay is required after forty hours of work in a workweek. Certain exemptions apply to specific types of businesses or specific types of work.

"The FLSA does not, however, require severance pay, sick leave, vacations, or holidays."

And that's basically what the law requires. We've interviewed people for the same position, with similar work history and education where there have been discrepancies in pay requests by as much as $40,000. Pay varies according to industry, experience, and environment. A great way to analyze what an industry pays is to visit www.payscale.com and order a free summary report of your salary comparison. We love this site. Answer a number of questions about the industry, position, title, location, size of company, education level, benefits received, and total compensation offered and then it compares you to your peers. In our case, to all of the other public relations directors with bachelor of science degrees in New York City who work for a company with six employees.

Fair wages are just the beginning. Money involves a lot more than the weekly paycheck. Medical benefits, disability insurance, expense accounts, car allowances, pensions, and retirement plans are extremely valuable to an employee and expensive to the organization. Here are a number of ways to make sure that money remains a motivator for employees:

- Make sure employees understand the cash value of their medical benefits. We cover health care 100 percent for each employee. In 2005, a single monthly premium cost $407 per month, almost $5,000 per year.

- Don't ask employees to cover business expenses on their personal credit cards or put out their personal money on the company's or manager's behalf. While working for very large companies, we both were asked to cover huge bills on behalf of the company for hotels, events, airline tickets, rental cars, and meals with the understanding that we would be reimbursed. It didn't matter that we would be reimbursed at some later date in the future, we didn't have the cash or credit to advance. Business travel became a weekly humiliation, with our management explaining why our personal credit issues required them to get us a cash advance for the trip.

- Retirement plans are a benefit, not a right. Again, make sure your employees understand the cash value of your corporate commitment.

tips: ten simple, cost-effective ways to show appreciation and earn goodwill

1. Training classes.

Sending employees to outside training classes is a win-win. They feel valued, love the day out of their routine, and you get back an enthusiastic employee with a new skill to offer the organization. Sarilee Norton, president of the Tru-Tech Business for Temple Inland, noticed a highly motivated member of her administrative support team. There were a number of personnel changes in her department, and the employee had stepped up to fill in. Sarilee wanted to do something to reward her extra efforts. The employee had expressed interest in Power Point, so Sarilee told her to find a one-day course in the area and sign herself up. She was thrilled and, when she returned, she began creating presentations for the management team—making a further contribution to the company.

2. Put nonmanagers in charge of noncritical projects.

Chris Colabella is the president of a construction leads service called CIS. Her staff loves to go on company outings—baseball games, picnics, Christmas parties. She hates planning them but is happy to have her staff appoint someone to lead the party effort. She assigns a budget and leaves the rest to them. The staff loves the responsibility of planning the events and contributing to the increased morale of the organization.

3. Acknowledge birthdays.

We love birthdays, but the celebrations can quickly get expensive and disruptive. Pick a gesture, set a budget, and do the same thing for everyone. If money is tight, a card signed by everyone in the department and a bouquet of inexpensive flowers is a nice gesture.

4. Try and think of rewards that are unexpected.
Sarilee Norton just may be the most clever rewarding manager we know. She's always trying to find ways to reward extra effort. She recommends you take a minute and really think about what will make people happy. She had an administrative manager who was going above and beyond. Her company often gets tickets to NASCAR events for customers who are escorted by her salesforce. When an extra ticket became available, she offered it to her administrative manager. Another win-win. He felt appreciated and the customers got the opportunity to meet the inside person who made sure their product was made and delivered on time.

5. Praise in front of the team.
Easy to do and makes people feel important.

6. Pampering.
We all love a little pampering. Think about gift certificates for a manicure or a massage, or tickets to a ball game, as a way of saying thank-you for a job well done.

7. The team lunch.
Consider throwing a pizza party when a big goal is reached. It's inexpensive and a great way for the team to bond and blow off some steam. If you have it on Friday, there's no reason that you can't splurge for a few beers, too. Yes, we're going against our no drinking rule here. If you choose to have a beer, make sure it doesn't get you drunk.

8. Bring junior people to networking events, business social functions, or along to meetings.

It's important for their career growth and feels like a big perk. Just make sure you prep them appropriately on what the event is, what they should wear, and what is expected of them.

9. Late-night etiquette.

If people are expected to work late and they are not eligible for overtime, it is important to acknowledge their additional effort. Make sure they have safe and free transportation home. Buy them dinner if they're working through the dinner hour. Make sure no one is alone or feels unsafe. Have employees escorted through dark parking lots. A good rule of thumb: If you wouldn't want your child or spouse put in the situation, you probably shouldn't put your employee in it either.

10. Inter- and intracompany recognition.

If there is a communication tool within your organization, make sure your team's successes are championed. State goals achieved specifically and name names.

girl talk

SHAR MCBEE, MOTIVATIONAL SPEAKER AND
AUTHOR OF *TO LEAD IS TO SERVE*

Shar McBee had not received any management training when suddenly she was put in charge of a staff of five hundred people. A wise mentor taught her a secret—think about what you can give, not what you can get. She tried it. Amazingly, it worked. Since then, Shar has taught the secret to thousands. In the 1980s Shar set out on a quest for deeper meaning. For ten years she traveled around the world working with relief organizations in a dozen countries. Today, Shar McBee is the president of SMB Publishing,

Inc. Her mission is to transform new managers into joyous leaders. She is currently working on the second book in her "Joy of Leadership" series. With an empowered group of people on your side, nothing can stand in your way. Shar shares her "secret" to motivating people with us.

Tell us about your philosophy and how you to came to it.
I was put in charge of a very large special event. I was responsible for five hundred people. I had a specific plan for how I wanted the event to be executed, and I shared it with the team. I thought I had prepared them for everything. What I hadn't prepared for was the fact that the event was massively oversold. We had thousands of people show up and nowhere to put them. My army of ushers was crumbling. They weren't seating people as I had trained them. They weren't being polite to the guests. They were herding them like cattle. I was beside myself. I started criticizing and trying to get this beleaguered force back in action. I was frustrated and angry. I went to my mentor, who had given me the assignment, and told her what I was dealing with and asked for advice. She asked me if I had given the ushers lunch. I was shocked. Of course I hadn't thought about it. All I could think about was what I needed. What I had prepared, my plan, and my plan in disarray. When I turned the situation around and started thinking about what they needed to get their job done, I was humbled. I started giving them support and encouragement and was amazed. Things turned around and they began working together as we had prepared. I teach people to come at things from the "give" side, not the "get" side. My whole joy of leadership method is based on the feeling that if you want to be happy, you want to be giving.

It sounds great, but how do we actually get on the "give" side?
First, stop thinking about how you can get someone to do what you want. Think always about what you can give for them to succeed. It's the most natural thing in the world. Look at nature. Nature is only giving and not getting. Take avocados. If you give that avocado seed to the earth, then it will give you a whole world of avocados.

I realize this is difficult. When you get under a lot of pressure or feel scared, you automatically contract. Here's another example. If you're stuck in a traffic jam, stop thinking, "How can I get out of here?" Think, "What can I give here?" Maybe all you have to give is your calmness. Maybe you can give people a break. Maybe you can give an inch and the traffic will actually open up.

Remind yourself that all people want is to do a good job.

Where do you begin?

The beauty of this is that you can begin immediately. It doesn't cost you time and it doesn't cost you money. It has to start with you. Most people want the other person to become giving. So first have a discussion with your team. Talk about your new philosophy and your own experience. Even people who are extremely skeptical eventually come around. The funny thing about giving is that it is energizing and not depleting. When you're being giving, you feel good. When you hold a discussion with a group of employees about this topic, the group is energized.

What is the benefit of giving?

Remember, the number one reason why people quit is not because of the work but because of hurt feelings. If you want to keep your workforce happy, then you're going to have to focus on what they need to be successful and give it to them.

The boss needs to be creative enough to take time to see if a project or task is right for an individual. Remember, delegating is not dumping. It's about giving people projects that are matched with their talents and sitting back and watching them succeed.

You say that your philosophy also applies to time management. How?

When people go wrong in this area, it's because they start focusing on the work instead of the people. Never forget that your number one priority is your people. It's very easy to lose sight of that. The really successful managers know how to support their people so their people can do the work. A lot of managers make the mistake thinking that the work is more important, but really, it's the people.

I remember going into a restaurant once, a big chain, and

they had a manager who was always totally stressed. He was constantly running around like a maniac, busing tables, writing checks, directing staff. He was nervous and his people showed the effects. Another time, I came when a different manager was on duty. She would sit at a corner table in the restaurant, looking as relaxed as can be. I wondered how she did it, especially given the other manager's frenetic pace. I sat down and asked her about it. "It's simple," she replied. "My job is supporting the team. I find out what they need and give it to them. I don't focus on the table that needs to be cleared. I focus on the people." She had more time because her people were operating more successfully.

delegation is not a dirty word

EMPLOYING YOUR EMPLOYEES

For some bosses, one of the most uncomfortable aspects of boss-dom is telling others what to do. The discomfort isn't entirely unwarranted; there *is* a delicate balance between assigning as much as possible to others and simply dumping your workload on those around you just because you can. But this is a balance every supervisor must overcome. You've earned the title of Lady Who Leads, and now you have to take charge and delegate responsibly and with respect for you and your employees.

Most of the time, sure, you could probably do it better and faster by just doing it yourself, but that doesn't allow your employees to grow, nor does it give you room to spread your wings and develop your own managerial and leadership skills. Make a plan and assign tasks thoughtfully, and everybody will win.

get over it!: how not to be afraid of your employees

A staggering percentage of leaders are scared of their staff. Have you ever had a manager who was never available when you needed her? Picked up her phone as soon as you knocked on her door? Missed staff meetings or let other people lead them? Are you such a manager?

Anxiety about facing the staff seems especially common among women—many of whom overcompensate and become the bitch bosses we have all encountered along the way up the ladder. It's not fair, but women bosses are judged more harshly than their male counterparts. We are socialized to accommodate, not confront, and when you are a manager, everything can feel like a confrontation. Women often feel self-conscious when assigning tasks, or uncomfortable when having to reprimand an employee. It is hard for many of us to find comfort in the "it's just business" mantra chanted by male professionals.

The upshot is that we often take too much on ourselves so we don't have to tell someone else to do it, accept mediocre work, get taken advantage of, or go overboard and mimic the male style of management, which is often dictatorial. This fear of confrontation can make it difficult to feel comfortable with your authority, get the best work from your employees, and efficiently manage the day-to-day delegation that is necessary to get your job done. So any way you look at it, if you want to be a good manager (and keep your job), you have to get over fearing your employees.

A few things to tell yourself before facing your staff:

- You were hired for a reason.
- Your skills are different than everyone else's, but obviously (since you got the job) a better fit for your position.

- Your boss has faith in you, so prove her right.
- You are not doing your employees a favor in the long run by accepting their mediocre work.
- You have skills and experience that are worth sharing with your staff.
- The employees need to prove themselves to you, too.
- You love this profession and you want to share your enthusiasm with your team.

no dumping!: how to delegate with respect

Delegating is assigning tasks, projects, and responsibilities with thought and with the understanding that you are there to offer support along the way. *Dumping* is handing off to-dos without explanation or guidance. Delegating without respect will quickly get you labeled as a bitch. And as women, unfortunately, we have to figure out how to hand off without pissing off. Don't assign anything that you wouldn't do or haven't done yourself; divas and prima donnas don't have a place in management. If possible, know how to do what you are delegating, even the littlest day-to-day tasks such as how to use the copier and call for messengers. "When assigning jobs to my employees, I try to see to the strength of the individual. Then I will entrust a project or a portion of a project for an employee to manage. This gives them a stronger investment in the job and the organization," says Susan Goldbetter, executive director of Circuit Productions, Inc.

Trying to put the task in a larger context for your staff is a learning opportunity. For instance, when telling your assistant that she needs to stuff a thousand envelopes for an upcoming client event, take two minutes to tell her about the goals for the event and how your team is the best group to achieve those goals. Treat every task with respect. Yes, boxing up and shipping out items is mundane and mind-numbing, but if you are unapologetic about assigning it—recognizing that it is crucial to your business—your employee won't feel embarrassed about doing it. Whenever possible, also explain how an assignment fits into her professional development. When it is time for the pre-holiday inventory, position it to the staff as a way for the team to become knowledgeable about the merchandise before the rush or telling your publicity assistant that labeling the two hundred envelopes going to book reviewers is a way for her to familiarize herself with key media names. What we know and need to share is that *the road to learning is doing*, and for those new to the business, they need to start by *doing* the basics.

Make sure your people have the tools they need to accomplish the job that they have been given. Be clear with your directions; for example, if you are asking someone to present at an upcoming conference, make sure you provide her with all of the relevant details, including subject, length of presentation, and audiovisual needs. Be available to answer questions and help with problem solving. If appropriate to the assignment, make other staff members available to help her. Be specific about your expectations, including due dates and, most importantly, how you will define success.

Again, there's no detail too small at the time of assigning. If instructing your assistant to set up a lunch meeting with a potential client, tell her where you want to go, the time you want to dine, and when you need it confirmed by.

Tamara Lawson, CFO for InnVest Real Estate Investment Trust, explains that "the only time I wouldn't delegate is if something is very time sensitive and important and it is faster to do it myself or if I am the only one able to do something. I find the latter is rarely the case, since I am always looking for opportunities to give the people who I manage the chance to develop new skills."

working together: it's all about the team

When delegating to a group, the assignment is usually more complicated than a few steps and will most likely involve several employees of varying levels of seniority. Your chances of a project going smoothly increase exponentially when you follow these steps:

- Set goal(s)/objective(s) for the team.
- Assign responsibilities and deadlines for senior team members.
- Meet with senior team members individually to divide the responsibilities into steps.
- Set progress meetings for the team.
- Be available for questions and assistance.
- Proactively check in with key employees to see how it's going; don't wait until the last second for a possible catastrophic surprise.

When assigning responsibilities, don't expect everyone to contribute the same; treat them and value them as individuals. To avoid conflict and tension within the group, clearly define both reporting procedures and individual responsibilities. And no matter what your feeling about a given project is, always show your staff enthusiasm and energy. Since you are the leader, the group looks to you for an emotional cue. If you are enthusiastic about it, then they will be, too. If you convey resentment or anxiety, then don't be surprised if the project becomes contentious or is executed in sub-par fashion.

be kind: why positive reinforcement works better than punishment

Fear and intimidation do not result in an efficient and motivated staff. In the short term you might get the attention you want from your employees, but in the long run they will be thinking about either how to get a new job or how to sabotage you. What's more, using fear as a management tactic is just plain lazy, a perceived shortcut to something that looks like respect but is something else altogether. It takes more time, focus, and commitment to manage without anger and/or negativity, but you will get more and better work out of your people. If you make it a point to criticize only in private, your staff will feel comfortable taking chances by sharing ideas at public meetings, learning new skills, and volunteering for the more complicated projects. If you take notice when someone has gone the extra mile by praising them publicly, then you will soon have a team willing to work late to get assignments done. If you reward employees who help one another out, then you will be leading a unified group. If you are enthusiastic and positive about your job, the company, and your staff, they will feel it. This reinforcement and support will both energize and motivate your employees in a way that fear and intimidation just can't.

SIX REASONS WHY YOU SHOULD, MUST, AND INEVITABLY WILL DELEGATE

1. The reality is that you simply can't do everything. Even if you want to.

2. You are not the best at everything; a good team should offer diverse experience and skills that complement yours.

3. You can't take on more unless you assign more.

4. If you don't delegate, you will limit your own professional growth and advancement.

5. You won't be honoring the unspoken agreement that you will teach and help your employees to grow.

6. It is just not good for the bottom line if someone with your skill set and wage is confirming appointments and mailing packages.

running a meeting: getting on the same page

Too many meetings waste everyone's time. If unstructured and undefined, a meeting is a wasted opportunity to get everyone on the same page. This is especially true of team meetings, where you have the attention of all of your people. There are a few tips for how to make the most of a meeting.

BE ON TIME!

Nothing is ruder than calling a meeting and then arriving late. We have all had that power-tripping boss who strolls in fifteen minutes after the meeting is to begin, getting off on the hushed audience. In addition to being rude, if your entire staff is waiting for you to show up, you're wasting a serious number of people-hours that could be spent being productive. This also holds true for employees who are constantly late. Everyone we spoke to says the same thing about this management problem: "Start without them." Walking into a meeting that is already in progress will hopefully be humiliating enough for your employee that he will make sure not to do it again.

HAVE AN AGENDA

Meetings that become a stream-of-consciousness exercise are a waste of everyone's time. Better to work out the topics and goals for the discussion prior to any sit-down. If you have an upcoming staff meeting, then create the agenda a few days prior and send it around so that your employees can come prepared. If you have a one-on-

one with an employee scheduled, then write the discussion topics down on a piece of paper for your personal reference. Having an agenda is especially important when you are facing a delicate conversation with a member of your team. In uncomfortable situations, it is a possibility that the conversation will quickly veer off-course and you may find yourself talking about the weekend instead of their tardiness problem. If you are meeting with a potential customer or client, then create the agenda at the office and review it just before the meeting. Planning what you are going to say in meetings large and small gives you control over the discussion and will help you achieve the mission behind the meetings.

TAKE NOTES

When you are going over a project or goals that have assignments attached, it is helpful for everyone to have it in writing. Assign one person to take notes in the meeting and e-mail them around to everyone immediately after the meeting. Make sure you review the notes before they are circulated to ensure that they include everything.

SENIORS FIRST

If you have a large department meeting, have a pre-meeting with the senior members of the team to assign topics of discussion. If there are sensitive issues raised, then you want to prepare seniors for how to follow up with their reports after the meeting. Caitlin worked for a publisher that was merging with another publisher. She and her colleagues were called into a company-wide powwow and told the news. Because the news was delicately and respectfully delivered and because, immediately following the meeting, the staff had one-on-ones with their managers, it was a smooth transition. It was obvious that senior people had been prepared, which made it better for everyone.

PUTTING A LID ON IT

There are those individuals who love the sound of their own voice. Piping up whenever possible, they can disrupt even the most well-organized gathering. Since we are beyond the days of raising our hands, the louder, more aggressive members of the team tend to monopolize meetings and it can be challenging for women to be heard. But as the manager, you need to move through the agenda and control the dialogue. Make it clear to those around the table when you want input and when you don't by limiting the number of times you request participation. If someone interrupts you, then look them in the eye and say, "In a minute, I'm not quite finished." Then, when you are finished, look back at the employee and give them permission to contribute with something along the lines of "You had something to add?" It is all about maintaining control of the discussion.

VISUAL AIDS

Use visual aids only when necessary. Why? They slow meetings down, distract the participants, and pull the attention off of you. Although on an emotional level it might be comforting to have a Power Point presentation between you and those in front of you, it isn't always the best way to deliver your message.

TIMING IS EVERYTHING

We've all experienced a meeting that was scheduled for an hour but stretched painfully into two. For the most part, long meetings are ineffective. By nature, we don't have the attention span to focus on anything for all that much time, especially if it isn't self-chosen. For team meetings try to stick to an hour, especially if brainstorming is required, because creativity often comes to a halt when people get tired. Take breaks if the meeting is going to stretch beyond two hours. Avoid scheduling meetings after lunch, when people are often in a food coma. And, if you want the undivided attention of the group, don't have a meeting toward the end of the day, when the staff will be thinking about their commute home or getting to day care on time to pick up their children.

OPPORTUNITIES ABOUND

There are opportunities for professional growth in team gatherings. You could use the weekly meeting as a chance for your junior staff members to practice public speaking. We both worked for someone who had new people present something during each Monday morning meeting. You could ask senior members to lecture on their areas of expertise. For instance, if you manage a clothing store, you could ask the buyer to present upcoming trends to the sales team.

HAVE A REASON

There should always be a reason for a meeting. If you want your staff engaged, then the topics for discussion should be specific and timely.

BE THE QUEEN

For many women used to hanging back in public situations, leading meetings can be scary. Even today, after several years of running our own business and several more years of managing, it is a little intimidating to face a table full of people. You are on stage at these meetings even if you are sitting down. But you need to embrace the role by sitting at the head of the table and projecting confidence even if you don't feel it and authoritatively running through the agenda. Whatever you do, don't let staff interrupt you. Ever. It shows weakness. And keep reminding yourself that you own the meeting.

reach for the stars: setting goals for your people

What keeps you motivated as an employee? Is it the promotion on the horizon? Is it the next big client? Is it for the personal accomplishment of mastering challenges such as public speaking, or will you simply not be satisfied until you have a corner office or make partner? Whatever the motivation, there is *something* that keeps you going, and since you have been promoted to a manager, then your employer has tapped into whatever it is that keeps you moving, looking forward, and contributing to the company's objectives. As a manager, you are responsible for using the team to achieve the goals of the company. The most efficient way to do this is by setting goals for your employees that will achieve the company's vision and at the same time tap into their needs and their vision for their career.

There are short-term goals and long-term goals for your employees. Short-term goals could include things like selling more of the blue T-shirts, writing the copy for the Memorial Day advertisement, baking one hundred corn muffins for the catering job, or ordering shipping supplies for an upcoming mailing. Long-term goals are usually those that merge the vision of the employee and the company, such as increasing sales of the T-shirt category by 20 percent over the summer, generating ideas for the holiday ad campaign, creating new menu items for the catering company, and developing a more efficient supply ordering and shipping system.

Keys for establishing effective goals for your people include not setting too many. Goals need to be achievable or you run the risk of undermining the confidence of your employees. The goal and the skills of the person to whom you assign it are in synch. Always position the goal in the context of the company's vision: The company is expanding its line of casual wear, so the increase in the T-shirt sales is the first step; the catering business is often rehired, so it is essential to have a diverse selection of menu items to keep returning customers from getting bored; the company gets 10 percent off on the costs of advertising in the local paper if they submit the copy early, so writing the holiday text early will save money. Most importantly, you need to generate enthusiasm for and commitment to the goal. So you want to position it as an important part of your employee's professional development.

good witch or big bitch?

YOUR BIGGEST FAN
Here's a story from our friend Paige Perkins:

I dropped out of my career when I had my son Evan, but after three and a half years I was ready to dive back in. At the time, I was developing an interest in improving education but was uncertain about how to get into it. Ellen, the headmistress of an academy in Massachusetts, wanted me to work at her school. She was quite persistent and, in part because of her reputation and belief in me, I agreed to come and work for her. After a year in the classroom and additional training, I became dean of this small but rapidly growing school. She was the absolute best boss I have ever had. Beyond being a leader, she became a mentor for me.

Why do you think she was a Good Witch?
I've never known anyone who thought me more able than she. She had (and expressed, without being sappy or insincere in any way) tremendous belief in my ability to do my job, and she let me know that. I found that hugely energizing, and it made me willing to confront and do some very hard things.

Another thing is that she was smart and knew what she was doing in most areas, so I knew I could rely on her judgment any time I decided to defer to her.

She was very clear about what her philosophy of education was, but she didn't force it on others. When push came to shove, she always stood up for what she believed in, but would always, if I disagreed with her course of action, take the time to calmly and very thoroughly explain her viewpoint, so that I understood where she was coming from. Since she had the entire school to think about (finances, building, personnel, educational quality, etc.), whereas I had only part (the educational quality), I almost always came to understand her course of action once I had enough information.

While we had some big disagreements at times about how certain aspects of the school should run, she never "pulled rank" on me, ever. She always took the time to help me understand a situation rather than just forcing me to do it her way.

Ellen tended to hire people to work for her who had a similar view of children and education. She was able to build a group of loving, cheerful people whom she held together through strength of purpose and was in communication with all of us at least once every couple of days. Each person was important to her and she let them know it. At the same time, she held extremely high standards of solvency, organization, professionalism, etc. She always thought first about the survival of the school, because without it no one in the group would have anything. Then all the details followed.

She delegated responsibility, and I think this is one of the key points of a good boss. It's what made working under her such a joy for me. My job was mine, not hers. I could call all the shots. If I got stuck and didn't know what to do in a situation, she would help me. She never forced me to do anything.

She was willing to teach the people under her, in a very quiet way, so they constantly got better and better at what they did. Then, at the same time, she could delegate more and more to them. This was, I believe, one of her most sterling qualities as a boss and one of the biggest keys to her success.

What did you learn from her?

I learned that:

- *My instincts are good, and if I just keep my cool, I can get a group of people to accomplish great things.*
- *Solvency is absolutely essential to an organization if it is to survive, and that this is an area an executive, has to constantly think about.*
- *Good leadership is not necessarily showy, but is accurate, caring, and ruthless about what's truly important.*
- *There is always something you can do, no matter what the situation. You just have to not get bent out of shape, calmly and analytically assess the entire situation, figure out what it is you can do, and then carry it out. By the time you're done, you'll have already figured out the next thing, and so on.*

Good Witch. Ellen didn't exhibit any of the Bad Boss Behaviors discussed in chapter 4. She was confident, led by example, didn't micromanage, respected the team equally, set achievable goals and reasonable expectations, treated people professionally, and had faith in their abilities. But more than that, Ellen became something that only one in a million managers can become . . . a mentor. Paige, more than twenty years later, attributes much of her own success as a leader to what she learned working for Ellen at the academy. That is one Good Witch.

direct and indirect reporting

If you find yourself in the unenviable position of having one of your staff treat their direct report badly, you are not alone. Dr. Dorri Jacobs, a NYC work issues coach, mediator, and internationally published author, advises, "In my experience, it is not a good idea to interfere, unless you are asked for help from your direct report, or when you observe that a major problem exists. Otherwise the perception of those involved is that the manager has no real authority." There is a very thin line between not interfering because you are respecting professional boundaries and being in collusion. If your direct report is beyond temperamental and leaning toward abusive, then you need to step in on behalf of the junior and the company. As a boss it is your job to train your staff, and maybe your direct report needs to develop her own management skills.

Whenever possible, don't step in between two staff members. Ilene Rosen, a mediator with a busy practice in Manhattan, offers the following strategy: "First discuss the problem with your direct report, explain why you are concerned, ask for his or her sense of what is going on, how best to resolve it, and if help would be appreciated. Get a time frame, if possible, for resolving the problem. Meet to discuss it after this, check on progress. Support your direct report, rather than take it over."

Beware of letting your ego get in the way here. It can be a boost to be the good gal in these scenarios, but by stepping in as the hero you are just generating more work for yourself. When you undercut the authority of your direct report, you are setting a precedent to have staff come to you with questions, issues, and problems. Taking care of someone else's support staff is far from your job. There is power that comes with your position, so you want to pass it along to the people who directly report to you, not take it away.

no chitchat: a guide to getting the most out of your together time

Unless you are unlikable or off-putting in some way—and we doubt that—then chances are that your employees will want to chat with you. A lot. As much as possible and for a variety of reasons. Maybe they feel the need to bond, maybe they are trying to get in good with you, maybe they are lonely, maybe they need to vent, or maybe they are just highly social. Whatever the reason is, you don't have that much extra time available for nonproductive chitchat. Even if you are swamped, keeping your door closed is not an option because you don't want to alienate your team. You also want your employees to feel comfortable talking to you about company issues, so staying unavailable isn't fostering that kind of environment.

Sometimes there is more behind the chitchat. There are those who are uncomfortable with face-to-face discussions and ramble rather than tackle an issue. What's the solution? Give everyone a few minutes where you are completely focused on what they are saying. During their few minutes, don't check e-mail, answer the phone, or peruse your date book. Think of it as their time. If they just needed to vent, then you heard them. If they wanted to bond with you, then you gave them a little of that. And if there is something more going on, then you can pursue it. When their few minutes are over, gracefully end the conversation, trying not to be too abrupt, or you may undo the good feelings you have generated.

girl talk

DIANE BATES, ENTREPRENEUR

Diane Bates cofounded Blue Sky Communications seven years ago. As the president of this busy public relations business, she has had the opportunity to manage employees at all levels. With an enviable zero percent turnover rate, Diane is clearly an excellent leader. In this Girl Talk, she shares the secret to her success.

What do you get out of managing on a personal and professional level?

Management is my favorite part of the job—especially as a business owner with twenty years experience in my field. It gives me a chance to cultivate new talent and teach people things I have learned in my career. Further, I've been managed by some individuals who were great at their job but poor managers as well as by some fantastic managers, and I've spent a lot of time considering the differences between the two. Specifically, what they did or didn't do to motivate me, teach me, inspire me, and help me stay excited about work. Management unto itself is a fascinating study in human behavior, and by simply relying on a substructure of principles—respect, honesty, communication, clarity of direction, the ability to recognize inherent strengths and weaknesses in different personalities, etc.—it can be easy and fun to groom people for success in their careers.

How have you evolved as a leader?

When we start out we operate mostly as tacticians and then leaders later on, so in the beginning I was more concerned with how well I performed in my job and the tasks at hand. But what I didn't know at the time was that my managerial skills were being cultivated by those managing me. Only in hindsight did those experiences—good and bad—come in handy. For example: I was repeatedly asked by a former boss to tend to her dog (walk him, feed him, baby-sit him, etc.)—she brought him to work every day. It seemed funny at first, but after a while it really undermined my self-respect at work. In fact, any time I was ever asked to run a "personal errand" for any boss, I did it with a smile but had an inherent understanding of the fact that it was simply wrong and showed a total lack of respect for me as a human being. Certainly this is standard operating procedure in the food chain of corporate America, but it is something I never, ever do with my staff. No one in my office handles personal chores for me. I'd be embarrassed to even ask them to!

An example of how good management influenced me was with a fabulous supervisor I once had who was amazing at deferring the glory of success to her team. She was the first to attribute our collective successes or jobs well done to "her fabulous team" and never, ever hogged the accolades to herself—it was incredibly motivating for me and, as a result, I never hog the glory or accolades now—in fact, I really could care less about that—but my staff being motivated—now that I care about because it means we will do good work, have low turnover, offer clients continuity, and all those good things that come from a happy staff. That impacts me and the business in a far bigger, more important way than any pat on the shoulder will. I know the accolades mean a lot more to our staff, so as far as I am concerned, they can have all the glory—it only makes our agency—and me, too—look great by association. That's why it's so important for managers to be aware of the impact their style will have on junior people as they rise in the ranks.

I have evolved as a leader through years of experience and having poor managers. I have also learned over time that one must always consider the ultimate best and worst possible outcomes of a situation and attempt to steer it toward the positive. This sometimes means your staff does not "see," understand, or agree with some of the decisions you make, but in business, one must always protect the business entity first—otherwise there will *be* no managers or employees.

TIPS FOR BEING A GOOD AND EFFECTIVE MANAGER
- Be accountable. A good manager doesn't expect, she inspects.
- Cover your back by always considering the ultimate best and worst possible outcomes of a situation and attempting to steer it toward the positive.
- We're all equal in the human race; thus people—regardless of their position in their job—deserve and need to be heard, to feel respected, and to have their individual talents and gifts celebrated.
- Get to really know them. At my agency we measure our employees' performance based on their individual talents, not some generic corporate template.
- Realize your influence. Many managers are unaware of the

impact their management style will have on junior people as they grow professionally.

- Rely on a substructure of principles like respect, honesty, communication, and clarity of direction, and trust your own ability to recognize inherent strengths and weaknesses in different personalities.

playing goddess

EVALUATIONS, PROMOTIONS, AND GIVING THE AX

Remember all those evaluations you had to sit through over the years? Your mouth shut tight while your superior listed all your shortcomings in clear, concise, and easy-to-decipher language? Well, now it's your turn to give the reviews, promotions, and yes, even the occasional pink slip.

Evaluations can be great learning experiences, for both you and your employees. They allow you to establish the big picture for each person on your staff and provide an opportunity to reenergize the employee and discuss her professional goals. If you want to get the inside scoop on what your employees really think of your job performance, let them turn the tables and put you to the test.

Promotions and raises are often the best parts of being a bigwig because they offer us the rare opportunity to be the good gal. On the other hand, you might find, as many bosses do, that the hardest part of your job is figuring out what to do when someone is just not working out. It can be tough, but if you follow the advice we share in "Got to Go: When Good News Isn't Good Enough" (page 145), you will survive and avoid traumatizing the surviving members of your team.

This chapter will give you the lowdown on performance reviews (what to do and what not to do, as well as a sample Performance Evaluation Form); how to turn bad news into good vibes; how to give (and get) constructive criticism; and how to let folks down easy when they don't quite cut the mustard.

day-to-day performance monitoring and feedback

If you were ever surprised by something raised during one of your reviews, you probably had a bad manager. Supervising another person is about the everyday flow of work. It is also about the tone and energy of the team. It would stand to reason that to pay proper respect to both of those aspects, you need to manage a little every day. Jennifer Kyle, a VP at a culinary publication, tells us "there are many scheduled internal and external meetings, but I also like to be available just to get things done more quickly without creating an unnecessary process." To open the doors of communication, start by checking in with your employees at least once a day and take the time to know a little about them. We had a boss who would sweep through the office in the morning without even a smile for those of us sitting in the "pit." At the end of the day, it left us feeling used, replaceable, and unappreciated and not like the precious resources we were.

Because it is your job to keep the flow of work moving along, when people come to you with questions, you should answer then as quickly as possible. If you don't have the answer at your fingertips, then get back to them later in the day, or let them know when to expect an answer. This is also true of reviewing documents. As a manager you most likely have a stack of reports, presentations, articles, and/or reviews sitting on your desk waiting for your changes/approval. Don't let them gather dust; people will either think it is okay for them to procrastinate or they will feel disrespected by you. Worse, if you are putting off changes, then you are stopping the flow of work and impeding those who report to you from doing their job.

If you are regularly checking in, you will also become aware of the things that are not getting done sooner rather than later. If you notice a task perpetually on an employee's to-do list, ask why. Maybe your person needs more direction, another set of skills, or maybe just a motivational nudge. This kind of daily monitoring (which we hasten to point out is not the same as micromanaging) will give you more control over what is getting done and when, and in turn a real sense of mastery over the workplace.

Make it your long-term goal to not bring up any new issue in the review with each of your employees. Instead, you should be letting them know whether or not they have succeeded in addressing any issues that you have already brought to their attention at the moment you noticed it. Not only does this avoid melodramatic reviews, but it is also a more effective means of managing: People are more apt to understand and respond to constructive criticism if it's presented at the time of a mistake or misstep, when the memory of what they did wrong is fresh in their mind as you discuss it with them.

why reviews are a must

As an employee you probably dreaded your review. Now as a manager, you probably dread it in a different way as you face stacks of evaluation forms. We not only want to encourage you to embrace the review process but we also want you to consider doing it more often.

The standard annual review gives you and your reports only one opportunity to set goals together, share feedback from clients and those above, tackle performance issues, and reiterate their role in the company's vision for the future. We worked for a company that had four reviews a year and only one was a salary review. This constant checking-in opened up communications between the manager and her staff. Sharon Rose, the owner of several clothing stores, says "without useful feedback, developmental needs, and a plan, it is very difficult to keep people motivated and make sure everyone is working with the same intentions."

Ideally, the evaluation should set out to review the quality of the work, communicate the expectations of the company, and open up discussions about the employee's own career goals. If you are planning on firing the employee, then the review also provides a formal documentation of their shortcomings and fire-able offenses. Conducting an honest review is crucial; if you fire someone after giving a glowing review, then you are opening yourself up to legal liability.

good witch or big bitch?

FAIR AND BALANCED, IT'S NOT JUST FOR FOX NEWS
Chris Colabella, president of Construction Information Systems (www.cisleads.com), is one of our mentors. She built her company from scratch and now has thirty-four employees in three states. She's read all of the management books, gone to trainings, and through years of trial-and-error, she's developed into an inspiring manager. She maintains a professional relationship with her staff and doesn't focus her energy on getting people to like her. She's fair; she listens to them and she tries to help them achieve their potential. And guess what? They like her, they really like her. Chris

does career development plans and performance reviews with all of her employees. She shares her program with us:

- Each employee has a written, clearly defined job description that I review with them two to three times per year. At these mini-reviews we go over strengths and weaknesses and discuss ways for them to improve. We also disucss their ambitions within the company.
- At the annual review, if they received a bad review, I felt that I was totally fair and justified in the evaluation. And I didn't feel like a bitch because they knew what was expected of them and how they were performing throughout the entire process.
- We then set a plan for what each person wants to achieve in the coming year as well as what I want them to achieve. This is the goal plan we use for the mini-reviews, and the process starts all over again.
- I taught my operations manager how to carry out the same process with her direct reports. Together we go through each written review before her meetings so she's comfortable with the system.

sample review

At our company, YC Media, we have instituted a Begin, End, Save, and Track review system—what we refer to as BEST. These four elements are summarized for each employee and provide both the starting points and framework for the review discussion. We like to give reviews twice a year, but only one is connected to raise consideration. The other is focused entirely on productivity and goal-setting. During this non-salary review, we also ask the employees to write up a performance evaluation of *our* management. While some might balk at this, we have found that more than anything else, it gives us a better idea of how the employees like to be managed. We have shared one of our reviews below (don't worry—we made a few changes; we don't want to embarrass any of our staff members!).

BEGIN

Three actions that we want the employee to start doing. We tie the Begin Actions to either short- or long-term goals for the employee. Again, these statements are a jumping-off point for a bigger dialogue about what we want to start seeing from our employee.

Sample:

- Attending more industry events
- Speaking up in team meetings
- Long-term planning for clients

END

Three actions or habits we want the employee to stop, sooner rather than later. We try not to include the really small foibles or ticks that drive us crazy, instead using this time to bring up issues that are serious enough to warrant 100 percent focus of both the manager and her employee. The Ends should be actions that directly affect her ability to grow in her career.

Sample:

- Missing deadlines
- Putting off the tough work
- Delegating time-sensitive tasks to your assistant

SAVE

Three actions that we want the employee to keep doing. When we get to this section of the review, we sigh in relief because we all have gotten through some tough issues. Again, we try to keep the focus on the big stuff here, because we have hopefully been pointing out good work on a weekly if not daily basis. So these are the action points that will get them a promotion and/or raise down the road.

Sample:

- Your creative input on client proposals
- Your attention to detail
- The quality of your writing

TRACK

These actions outline a plan for the employee to track his growth in the Begin section of the review. They also spell out what success looks like to us—we want you to begin A, so if we see B, you have succeeded. Since the Track items are a starting point for the discussion, we then work together with the employees on achieving these goals.

Sample:

- Attend two industry events a year.
- Contribute one comment per team meeting.
- Show me your proposed campaigns for each client so I can help you, if you need me to, with the planning.

five common evaluation mistakes

NOT ENOUGH SPECIFIC EXAMPLES

Both positive and negative review statements are more impactful when backed up by specific examples. "You tend to miss deadlines" is easier to dismiss than "You have a habit of missing deadlines. Last month the new business proposal I asked you to draft for soy yogurt wasn't on my desk until four days after it was due to the potential client, June's status report wasn't delivered until the middle of July, and your final edits to the black raspberry jam press release were two days late." If you put criticisms in a context during the review, it will force the employee to think twice about her past and future performance. Likewise, positive reviews, when backed up by specific examples, help motivate your staff. "Your clients all seem to like you" is nice to hear, but wouldn't it be better to say "I have had many calls from the marketing director at Regent Restaurant Group and Wellbeing Spa both telling me how thrilled they are with your results."

GOALS ARE TOO VAGUE

If you set a goal for a sales rep to "increase sales," that is open to interpretation. But if you tell her that you want to see a 5 percent increase, there is no disputing whether or not it's been achieved.

NO CONTEXT

To help develop your employee's big picture thinking, review all of the roles she has in the company. She needs to know that while keeping customers happy is a crucial part of her job, so is also being a mentor for her direct report. While she does need to be focused on the sales goals for the Main Street clothing store, she also needs to start being tuned into the company's overall sales goals.

TOO NEGATIVE

If you barrage someone with criticisms, two things will happen. They will stop hearing you and they will—out of self-preservation—convince themselves that you are wrong. We recommend that if you are reviewing someone you want to keep and develop, then keep your criticisms brief and concise. Balance criticisms with good news while providing action steps for fixing the problems. Reassure them that you are committed to turning it around with them.

It is easier to deliver good news, but if you spend the review patting the backs of your employees, then you are missing an opportunity to help push them to the next level. If you are not sharing with your subordinate the road map to a promotion, you are robbing her of her professional development.

the word

A TRUE MENTOR FROM ABIGAIL DISNEY, FOUNDER AND PRESIDENT OF THE DAPHNE FOUNDATION

The best manager I have ever met is Gerry Laybourne, formerly of Nickelodeon and then Disney, now of Oxygen Media. She has built an empire of rabidly loyal employees who would lie down on the train tracks for her because of a rule that would be in many other places totally radical: She is the queen of nice. She is nice to waiters and busboys and secretaries and senators and princes and little old ladies on the bus. She is absolutely militant about the power of niceness, and she is walking proof that as a life strategy not only does it work, but it creates an aura of contentment and clarity around the person who practices it and everyone around them. It is an extraordinary thing, and brave, since this is not a doctrine supported by most of those in the Fortune 500. She is a hero.

the good news: turning bad news into better employees

Let's say that one of your event planners is loved by the clients but has a gruff manner with outside vendors that results in complaints from the caterer, florist, and band. Even if they begin raising their fees when she is on the case, it would be better to keep her and work through her challenges. You would not wait until review time to address the issue, so you would jump right in by setting up a one-on-one with her. Begin the discussion by providing the event planner with an overview of the problem, using specific examples to back it up. Juli Tolleson, an account director at US Concepts, would then "ask her perspective on the problem, then explain clearly and constructively what could have been done to make it more effective. I also ask what I can do better in the future to support her so that she can do a better job." When good employees go bad, there is usually a reason for it and often it is a simple case of not having what they need to get the job done. Sarah Barns, a sales representative for a computer company, tells us that sometimes the hard talks can turn things around with a disappointing employee. "I had a junior-level employee who really shined in the interview process and then fell apart quickly after starting. We realized it about three months into her employment and figured we would let her go but gave her a warning and continued through a full warning process and, honestly, never thought she could turn it around. But she did. Apparently she needed more direction than we realized and talking everything out really helped."

got to go: when good news isn't good enough

Unfortunately you will have to fire people, and even if they are the worst employees ever, firing anyone is a drag. Janie Kleiman, senior vice president of television production for 20th Century Fox Television, concurs: "The only aspect of my position that I find not enjoyable is when an employee has to be replaced. We are all dependent on our jobs to support our families and maintain our health benefits. Some people need their jobs, as their jobs identify who they are and have become part of their personality. I take it very seriously when I have to fire or replace someone."

The bad news is that it is part of your job, so—no excuses—you must wield the ax. It would be best for both of you if the employee quit, so indicate at the verbal warning stage that things are not looking good, then at the written stage reiterate that the situation is looking dire. Concrete examples of missteps will close the door to a discussion. At this point, hopefully the employee will take the hint and pack her bags. It is far less ugly if she gives her notice. If, however, she refuses, fails to be realistic, and doesn't change, then you are going to have to do it for her. Firing someone is one situation as a manager that will forever cast you, in that person's mind at least, as a bitch. The best you can hope to do is retain your dignity and treat your soon-to-be ex-employee with respect. Invite her into your office, sit her down, list the reasons you are firing her by reading from past reviews and warnings, and ask her to leave the building that day. Why should she leave that day? Because she could become destructive or cause the remaining team to feel anxious, guilty, resentful, or fearful. This is where it can get really messy, because she will need to be escorted out. Check with HR, because you might have to enlist the security department to accompany the ex-employee out the door, with only a pit stop at their desk to grab personal belongings. She will need to leave any and everything that belongs to your company. (See "The Word," page 147, for more tips on firing.)

To make this as easy as possible for all concerned, don't give the employee an opportunity to be emotional. If you are apologizing for what you have to do, or waiting for her to let you off the hook by telling you it is okay, then you are leaving room for her to cry, scream, or throw something. Another way to make sure it doesn't escalate is by giving honest feedback along the way so you are not surprising her with anything new. Deliver the news quickly and succinctly, and don't take responsibility for things turning sour. If you did your job right and offered suggestions and methods for solving the problems, then she owns this, not you. "I fire someone when I have warned them, and given them a chance to save themselves, but they either don't have the ability to do the job or they just don't care enough. There are too many good, hardworking, smart people to have any mediocre people around," shares promotions director Frances Miller.

the legal word

LAURIE MALKIN, ATTORNEY

Laurie Malkin is an Associate in the Employment and Employee Benefits Department of Schulte Roth and Zabel LLP. Among her responsibilities, Laurie counsels employers on employee hiring, management, and termination; discrimination and harassment; disability and leaves-of-absence issues; restrictive covenants; and wage and hour laws. Laurie also negotiates employment contracts and severance agreements, and she litigates and arbitrates employment disputes before federal and state courts, administrative agencies, and arbitral tribunals when amicable resolution is not an option.

If it looks like an employee is well on his or her way to being fired, can you take us through the typical process from a legal point of view?
Start the process well before firing is imminent.
This is the most important step. When I advise an employer about whether to terminate someone's employment, I start by asking three questions:

1. Why do you want to terminate the employee's employment?
2. Is the employee a member of one or more legally protected

classes? The most common federal legally protected classes include race, color, religion, sex, national origin, age, and disability. Many states and localities also prohibit workplace discrimination on such bases as marital status, sexual orientation, and arrest record.

3. Does the employer have clear, consistent, and contemporaneous documentation of the employee's poor performance or other reason for firing?

When the answer to the second question implicates membership in a legally protected class, and/or when the answer is yes to the second question and no to the third question, then the employer should proceed very, very cautiously. Its potential exposure to legal liability—regardless of any other facts relevant to the situation—is heightened. "Proceeding carefully" usually means consulting legal counsel right away. It also means considering whether to offer the employee at issue a severance package (money) in exchange for the employee's written promise that he or she will not sue the company.

This brings me to a corollary suggestion: As a general rule, I do not recommend that an employer offer any terminated employee—particularly one who is fired for poor performance or misconduct—any severance pay, paid continuation of health benefits, or other remuneration to which he or she is not otherwise entitled under the law, without first obtaining a legally binding promise in writing from the terminated employee releasing the employer from legal liability. In most cases, unless the employer has a policy stating otherwise, there is no legal duty to provide severance pay. Yet, employers often pay employees (even those fired for misconduct) severance pay, only to have the same employees use severance payments to hire lawyers who then demand *more* money, threatening to sue.

Consider whether the employee is employed "at will" or is subject to a contract for employment.

Another key initial consideration when deciding whether to fire someone is asking if the employee has a legally cognizable employment contract or, instead, is employed on an "at will" basis. Keep in mind that, generally, private employment in the United States is "at will" absent a valid, usually written, employment contract establishing otherwise. "At will" employment means that either the employer or the employee can terminate the employment relationship at any time, for any reason, with or without notice or cause. There are a few exceptions to the "at will" rule. The most notable exceptions are laws that prohibit discrimination against employees because they belong to legally protected classes (e.g., race, ethnicity, sex, age, religion, disability), laws protecting whistleblowers, and other public policy exceptions. Also, certain states such as California construe more narrowly "at will" employment, providing broader protections for employees than in other parts of the country.

Employers often ask whether they must explain to the terminated employee the rationale for their employment decisions. Although sharing such information may be advisable, when employees are employed "at will," it often is not necessary to provide a detailed explanation. Non-unionized employees who work for private employers have no inherent workplace "due process" rights absent a contractual obligation, usually in the form of an employment contract or employee handbook, stating otherwise. Nor do employees have any implied right to confront their bosses or others who have accused them of wrongdoing.

Conduct an exit interview and protect company interests.
Employers always should conduct an exit interview for each employee who leaves his or her job. The exit interview often is only a very short meeting. During this exit interview, the employer should take the following steps:

1. Make sure that the terminated employee has returned all company property—computers, computer passwords, client and contact lists, keys, letterhead, credit cards, etc. In fact, if you suspect an employee of wrongdoing, or if the employee has had access to sensitive or proprietary company information (or comparable personal information about you), you

may want to limit the employee's access to the company, to other employees, and particularly to company computers, e-mail systems, and other electronic resources, even before you terminate employment. Theft of trade secrets and propri-etary information, and malicious destruction of computer files or other company property, poses serious risks to today's employers.

2. Advise the employee of any applicable duties concerning confidentiality of company information and restrictive covenants. In some cases, the employer may limit the em-ployee's ability to set up or work for a competing operation, to solicit company clients, or to solicit for employer or hire company employees. The laws concerning noncompetition and nonsolicitation agreements are complex and state specific. The employer, therefore, should discuss such matters with legal counsel before the exit interview.

3. Advise the employee about his or her rights to continue health and other benefits. Under federal and state laws, many employers are required to not only offer continued medical benefits at the employee's expense, but also to notify the ter-minated employee of his or her rights to such continuation coverage.

4. Tell the employee when he or she will receive the final pay-check, and tell the employee what this paycheck will include. States vary on how final payments must be made. In some cases, employers must pay employees everything they are owed on the last day of work. In other states, payments can be made on the next regular payday. Also, in some cases, em-ployers must pay terminated employees for accrued, unused vacation. For all of these reasons, it is important to check with your HR department or employment attorney.

5. An exit interview also often is the perfect time to ask ques-tions. Departing employees often can be a valuable source of information about what you, as an employer, are doing right or wrong.

disciplined disciplinarian: being consistent, fair, and constructive

Mistakes are always a learning opportunity for both you and your employees, so make the best of the discussion you will inevitably be having with your subordinate. Set aside a time to speak to your person as soon as the mistake happens. Outline beforehand the points you want to make and specific suggestions for how the task or situation could have been handled better. During the meeting be calm, clear, and unemotional. After you have presented the issue, listen to what she has to say. Is she pointing out challenges that are affecting her ability to do her job? Does she need additional training? Is she just unwilling to accept responsibility? If she seems willing to work on it and is onboard with making changes, then work with her to create a clear list of steps to turn the problem around.

when good people leave

Prepare yourself, because it's going to happen and you can't take it personally. Good employees will outgrow you at some point, be recruited, or will want your job. Leah Andrews, a restaurant manager, said "I knew what was happening as soon as Cheri asked if she could come into my office and proceeded to shut the door behind her. All I wanted to do was fall on the floor, scream NOOOOOOO, and cry like a baby." Any manager knows what a blow it is when a great person leaves. It impacts the equilibrium of the team, since everyone was in a groove of working together. It puts more work on the plates of several of the team members, including the manager. There is the pressure to hire someone "just like" them or at the very least find someone great right away. It distracts you and several members of the group from meeting their goals. And on an emotional level, if you cared about the employee, then you will miss her. Unfortunately (and fortunately) there are just too many opportunities these days for people to stay long periods of time at any one company.

If you think that she is worth fighting for, then by all means give it a go. Check with HR and *your* boss about what you can counter offer in salary and/or promotion. That said, you should also be aware that counteroffers are not always appreciated. How many times did you give notice only to be told that the company "really wants to keep you" and suddenly your supervisor had the funds to pay you more? How did that make you feel? It makes most of us really angry, but not as angry as no counteroffer would make us. So do the dance and offer more, but don't expect it to work.

The best you can do is prepare yourself for the likelihood of it happening at some point. It behooves you to think ahead and plan for each strong employee's departure by staying in the loop, having at least a basic understanding of their job responsibilities, and preparing yourself mentally for the possibility of doing much more work yourself until you find a replacement. If your staff works directly with accounts, then commit yourself to some face time with each of the accounts so that in the event someone leaves, they will still feel taken care of by a representative of the company. If the departing employee works in shifts, make sure that you have a plan for juggling schedules should an employee no longer be available. If she travels to attend trade shows or conferences, then make your peace with the fact that you might have to go on the road at some point until a replacement can be found.

boy talk

David Craig, television and film executive, has worked for six high-powered women during his career. Being successful while navigating the competitive waters of the entertainment business is not easy. We spoke to him about his experiences working for women.

Tell about any common challenges you noticed your female bosses dealing with in the workplace. And how they overcame them.

The common challenge seems to be their interactions with men in positions above them, especially if the man is less qualified than they are for the position. This still seems to happen frequently in business, even in TV and film, and it is very frustrating and the usual response is to remain professional and operate as if this were not the case. The interesting thing that I have not encountered is much struggle that these women have balancing their work and home lives. They can either afford to hire home help or have kids already off at school or grown or somehow manage to handle both aspects of their lives without sacrificing their ambitions at work.

Do you think women or men make better bosses?

The answer is mixed. Because I've had strong relationships with women in my family, I've tended to feel that I could work better with women and felt more supportive toward them as they made their way in male-driven industries. That said, I've had the misfortune of working with some of the most ruthless, competitive, and nonsupportive women in both film and publishing. One of the things I found difficult was expecting a more compassionate or sensitive approach toward people management, which has backfired. In many cases, the more difficult women bosses worked very hard to eliminate any softer side to their management. In my opinion, they were trying to overcompensate for being pitted against men in higher positions; however, these same women had no qualms about exploiting their sex appeal to achieve favors or benefits from men. This has always struck me as a contradiction in a political sense for women's rights. What these tougher and more successful women (both the better and worse bosses) have taught me is that the work environment is not about gender politics and they do not want to be seen as role models. For them, business is war and all is fair in war and work.

Female/boss character traits that worked well for you?

For those bosses who were more supportive and less threatened by me, I've been able to grow as an employee and help build the company more successfully than if I had been held back. In exchange, I've willingly offered more loyalty and support, which has resulted in a couple of long-term jobs working for these more supportive female bosses. Their support proved mutually beneficial.

Did you have a favorite female boss?

I've actually had two great female bosses. One was film producer Marcia Nasatir, who, despite forty years seniority, treated me as an equal from the first day and allowed me to participate in all aspects of the company. The other great boss was television executive Delia Fine, who has helped me enormously with navigating the waters in my first corporate position and helped me use my strengths to better advantage.

culture is queen

CORPORATE CULTURE 101

Corporate culture is the heart and soul of an organization and guides how employees act and feel. It is comprised of values, ethics, and aesthetics. Company values, dress code, phone manners, and benefits policies all fall under the umbrella, and a corporate culture can be stated or understood. For example, YC Media has a very casual office dress code, yet it's understood by all of our employees that when outside guests or clients are coming in, then everyone must "dress up" for the occasion.

Corporate culture can be prescribed from the beginning or evolve over time. It generally reflects the founder's ethos but adapts as a company matures and grows. Sure, the animators at the Walt Disney Company stopped wearing jackets and ties to work every day, but the company still stays true to the core mission that Walt himself began of providing quality entertainment for people around the world.

Dr. Randall Hansen, webmaster of Quintessential Careers, as well as publisher of its electronic newsletter, *QuintZine*, writes a biweekly career advice column, "The Career Doctor," and teaches at Stetson University in Florida. He believes that assessing how well you will fit into a corporate culture will be a strong indicator of your happiness and success in a job. On his Web site, he recommends you interview other employees in a company to get a real picture of the culture. Dr. Hansen's questions are good to consider when interviewing for a new position or assessing your own corporate culture:

- What ten words would you use to describe your company?
- What's it really like to work here? Do you like it here?
- What's really important?
- How are employees valued?
- What skills and characteristics does the company value?
- Do you feel as though you know what is expected of you?
- How do people from different departments interact?
- Are there opportunities for further training and education?
- How do people get promoted?
- What behaviors get rewarded?
- Do you feel as though you know what's going on?
- How effectively does the company communicate to its employees?

what defines your corporate culture: balancing standards and style

We all want the perfect workplace—a bright, happy environment full of productive and motivated workers whistling while they work. Creating and maintaining such a place requires thought and discipline. At the heart of happy companies are happy people. Creating a culture dedicated to employee happiness is one way to ensure success. And it starts with some basic premises. Pay people fairly, if not better than the industry standard. Create a benefits package that takes the entire worker's needs into consideration. Be clear about goals for the company and individuals and communicate with them on a regular basis.

Most of the women we interviewed acknowledged that their corporate culture and management style work hand in hand. Gretchen Monahan, owner of six Grettacole salons and spas in the Boston area, described her 110 employees as a family and talked about how they support her and she supports them. Claire Burke, senior vice president at Hunter Public Relations in New York City, explained how people in her organization who care more about their job titles than their job responsibilities won't last. "My clients don't even know my title," she said. "My team always feels bad when we're in a meeting and the client introduces me as their 'account supervisor.' But for senior management, getting the work done is the priority, not throwing around our titles and position."

Company values shouldn't be all talk, but rather the guiding philosophy that employees know and integrate into their work lives. Not surprisingly, the best companies to work for do this the best. Wegman's chain of supermarkets was voted the number one company to work for in 2005 by *Fortune* magazine because of their unusual mission, "Employees first, customers second." The Wegman's family rationale has always been when employees are happy, customers will be too. And they put their money where their mouth is: They pay their staff more than their competition, and in an industry characterized by either strong unions or no benefits at all, health care is offered to all employees, part-time and full-time.

To determine which companies are best, *Fortune* magazine has developed a four-part evaluation that contributes to one-third of the overall score. We think it is a good matrix to use when evaluating your own culture. *Fortune* looks at credibility (communication to employees), respect (opportunities and benefits), fairness (compensation, diversity), and pride/camaraderie (philanthropy, celebrations).

How do you want your employees to feel when they walk through the door? How do you communicate with your employees? Does everyone "feel the touch" of senior management? Are opportunities for growth and benefits competitive with or better than industry standard? Is your workplace fair? Do you pay people the same or better than the industry standard? Is your workplace diverse, including people from all different backgrounds? Does the company make employee career development a priority? Does the workplace make philanthropy a priority? Do they care about more than their own bottom line?

Only when you have considered all of these questions and put a positive workplace culture in place can you be assured that your good employees won't leave as soon as a better opportunity comes along.

what do you stand for?

Assessing, articulating, and then living your brand values will be challenging. It will also be the most important thing a company can do to create a consistent culture for their team to thrive. At YC Media, we value client service above all else. We created a laid-back but professional workplace, champion individuality, and offer work-hard-and-then-the-sky's-the-limit career opportunities.

Most corporate Web sites list their mission statement and values. We read through a number of them when researching this chapter, and our favorite by far is Yahoo!'s. Check it out at http://docs.yahoo.com/info/values/.

Keep in mind that you are not the only one thinking about values. Potential employees are thinking about them too. As a matter of fact, university career counselors suggest that job candidates assess their own values before even seeking employment. The career board Web site from the University of New South Wales in Sydney, Australia, suggests students make a list of values that are important to them and offer samples. They suggest students look at extrinsic values, including, wealth, power and prestige, security, status, recognition, and perks and bonuses; intrinsic values such as achievement, honesty, compassion, ambition, and personal and intellectual growth; contextual values like organization size, indoors or outdoors, aesthetically pleasing, varied versus same; and people issues, including teamwork and independence.

the word

TESSA JANE GRAHAM, BRAND STRATEGY CONSULTANT

Tessa Jane Graham is a founding partner of Fresh Partners (www.fresh-partners.com), a company dedicated to developing personality-led brands and businesses. Fresh Partners grew from the work Tessa did with celebrity chef Jamie Oliver as the director of strategic development. Under her leadership, Jamie's business expanded to forty-six countries and twenty-three languages, and he has sold over twelve million books worldwide. Her experience developing global brands includes previous stints with Joe Boxer, Red Sheriff, and Razorfish, the digital consultancy where she worked with a variety of global clients. She's been based in Canada and the United States, and is currently in the United Kingdom, where she is a brand consultant.

Tessa shares her experience in developing a corporate culture, managing her team, and managing the trials and tribulations of a new business.

- As a branding person, I feel that understanding an organization's brand is key to being able to be a good manager. If everyone on the team understands the vision and the mission as well as the role that they can have in reaching these goals, everyone is focused in the same direction. Done right, the brand influences everything that the company does, most importantly its corporate culture. The team then understands what their common goal is and everyone, ideally, works toward this.
- I've always thought that transparency in management is the best practice. Sharing with the team where things are, what could be better, what the numbers look like, how people are feeling—this way there are no secrets and no hidden agendas. Everything is out in the open.

casual friday: why a dress code works

Cynthia Rowley is an acclaimed fashion designer with stores all around the world. She is also the creator of Swell, a national lifestyle brand, with writer Ilene Rosenzweig. She has a strict dress code for new employees and interns that was developed after one too many run-ins with bad outfits and bare midriffs. After all, one person's personal style can become your nightmare.

Judith Glaser tells a story of her experience with the Donna Karan dress code policy when she was consulting for them in her book *Creating We: Change I-Thinking to WE-Thinking and Build a Healthy, Thriving Organization*:

> In 1996, the day before my first visit to Donna Karan International to meet Donna and her senior leadership team, I spent a lot of time

thinking about and planning what I would wear. At the time I did not own one piece of her line of clothing, although I would have loved to. At the time, I would buy designer clothes only when they were on sale, and I did not have a favorite designer. From time to time I shopped at designer outlets to find my "status apparel," which I proudly wore to appropriate parties. While I almost became a designer out of high school, that was long ago. My design instincts for apparel had given way to my instincts for helping executives create the future of their businesses, and I was okay with the trade-off, until I met Donna Karan and her thirty-one senior executives.

The suit I chose for my first visit was quite beautiful: a taupe and white wool with an Italian designer's name on the label—someone I never bought from before, or after. It had a Chanel look and, in my mind, I was dressed appropriately for the occasion. . . . As the door opened, I got the shock of my life. It took a few seconds to fully sink in.

There I stood—all alone—in my beautiful taupe suit, surrounded by two dozen executives all wearing black—black suits, black pants, black tops.

Judith later found out that Donna required everyone to wear black, because other colors infringed upon her creativity. She wanted a monochromatic backdrop to design. Not knowing the dress code put Judith at a disadvantage; her outfit screamed "outsider" as she walked through the door.

But a dress code isn't just about fashion and for people in the fashion business. It's about fitting in, being appropriate, and representing. Styles of dress change from business to business and city to city. Frankly, a clearly defined dress code would be a relief from the many hours of outfit anxiety we've all experienced trying to figure out what to wear to a big meeting, presentation, or the first day at a new job. When Kim was at her first job in New York City, she had no appropriate clothes—only she didn't know it until years later when a group of people had gotten together to laugh about old times. Her "business girl" outfits got the biggest chuckle—more specifically, the fuschia rayon pants suit with a matching scarf and straw hat (give her a break, it was 1990 and she's from New Jersey). What worked when she was a sales associate at the Casual Corner in Colorado most definitely didn't work in the halls of a design magazine in New York City. So, how do you define a reasonable dress code policy?

The Small Business Association's online Women's Business Center (www.onlinewbc.gov) offers guidelines for employee dress code and sample language for your employee handbook. "As an employee of XYZ, we expect you to present a clean and professional appearance when you represent us, whether that is in, or outside of, the office. Management, sales personnel and those employees who come in contact with our public, are expected to dress in accepted corporate tradition. A specific list of suggested do's and definite don'ts, including a detailed definition of business casual, is available from your personnel representative and will be posted in each work area.

"It is just as essential that you act in a professional manner and extend the highest courtesy to coworkers, visitors, customers, vendors, and clients. A cheerful and positive attitude is essential to our commitment to extraordinary customer service and impeccable quality."

But is that helpful? What is "accepted corporate tradition"? Make it easy for your team and yourself. Be as specific as possible. Never say, "Please dress up, we have to meet a new client tomorrow." Instead, be specific: "Suits" or "No blue jeans." If you're a small enough organization, do what we do, and recommend a specific outfit of theirs that you've noticed that would be appropriate for the occasion.

In absence of a clearly defined dress code, pay attention. What do your superiors wear? Think about where you're going and who you're going to see. Nothing zaps your confidence faster than feeling or being accused of being inappropriately dressed.

After winning the national championship, the undefeated Northwestern University Women's Lacrosse Team was invited to the White House to meet the president. When their photo with the president was published on the Web, offers came pouring in from media outlets for interviews. How great for women's lacrosse that a national media outlet such as the *Today* show was suddenly interested in their sport. Unfortunately, they weren't interested in women's lacrosse or even women's sports for that matter. They wanted to interview the members of the team who wore flip-flops to meet the president. That was news—not that the women had gone 21–0 during their season, but that they had gone to Ann Taylor and purchased a sun dress and matching thongs (shoes, not underwear) and wore that for a photo with the president of the United States.

the dress code that goes everywhere

After years of "*Glamour* don'ts," we've created the dress code that goes everywhere:

- When in doubt, go black. A black pants suit, a black dress, a black skirt with any kind of top, works everywhere for every occasion. Throw in some black shoes, and without even thinking, you're perfect.
- Natural fibers always. Stay away from rayon, acetate, or anything shiny. With wool and cotton you can never go wrong.
- Grooming goes a long way. Get a regular manicure or do it yourself. Nude lasts longer and the colors have better names. We like "Naked Truth" in the winter and "Iced Chai Latte" in

the summer. Keep your eyebrows waxed, threaded, or plucked. Keep hair split-end free, and when overdue for a haircut or color, just pull it back into a ponytail.

- Shoes make the woman and there's a pair to fit any size—something you cannot say about expensive designer jeans. Keep your shoes in good condition. Get soles and heels repaired and keep them shined. Especially boots.
- No bare midriffs, ever. We love tank tops and hate tummies.
- Unless you've got the legs, save the miniskirts for the weekend.
- Wear day clothes during the day, and evening clothes at night. We worked with a woman who wore taffeta skirts with matching shoes and halter tops to work, and we could never figure out if she hadn't gone home the night before.
- Check out the magazines. We love *InStyle*'s fashion coverage. They give you a number of options for all shapes, sizes, and budgets.
- Wear makeup—you will look better. It doesn't have to be heavy, just a little foundation, blush, and mascara will do the trick.

good witch or big bitch?

The Devil Really Does Wear Prada

Some corporations champion their bad behavior. Long before the book *The Devil Wears Prada* came out, it was common knowledge that editors who worked at Condé Nast magazines were mean bitches and even called themselves "Condé Nasties." The sad truth was that not only was human resources privy to the misery—they perpetuated it. Krista Dale was a young editorial assistant with almost four years of experience when a magazine sale found her interviewing for a job at Condé Nast. After failing the requisite typing test (on a typewriter, by the way), she was told by the human resources manager that "she had no skills," and was offered a position as the second editorial assistant to the editor in chief of a fringe magazine for more than $10,000 *less* than the $28,000 she was making at her last position. When asked how people could survive on that kind of income, the human resources manager told her that "her editorial assistants didn't work because they needed the money." Hey, at least she was honest.

Know the culture you're going into. Learning a new job is hard enough without the added pressures.

starting from scratch: challenges and opportunities for the entrepreneur

It's really exciting when you start a new business—there's nothing but upside. You can create the kind of culture you always wanted to work in. It's your party now, and (if you're lucky) no one will be crying. Here's a list of questions to ask when starting up:

- How am I going to communicate with my employees and how often?
- What is their office space going to look like?
- How much does the competition pay for the same job?
- What kinds of benefits does the competition offer?
- What does the company value and how are you going to communicate it with the team?

fish out of water: culture clash hurts more than feelings

A woman from the Northeast began working for a company based in the Midwest. In her past jobs, venting was the order of the day. Employees were free to express their opinions. Comments were made, critiques given and received, stress relieved, and both sides of the confrontation/conversation walked away knowing that the product would be better for their disagreement. Nothing was taken too personally, and things said in the moment were accepted as just that. She thought this was the way the industry worked. Unfortunately, she found out much too late that what worked in a deadline-heavy, fast-paced New York environment just didn't play in Peoria. Her new midwestern culture had fewer deadlines and a much different way of communicating. Direct criticisms were just not made. And there was no such thing as things said "in the heat of the moment." The midwesterners characterized their communication as more civilized. New Yorkers would call it fake. And most would agree that when you can't face problems directly, you'll have a hard time effecting change.

But, any way you cut it, the idea that people from different parts of the country and world communicate differently is not stereotypical or overplayed. You don't have to actually speak a different language to be speaking a different language.

the word

Amie Malkin moved from the United States to London more than four years ago. She has been on the front lines of cultural difference and offers a few pieces of advice:

- Any American coming over to Europe should plan to spend more time listening and less time talking. It's impossible to overstate how much you can learn from your colleagues and their infinite differences.
- In practical terms, this also means giving your colleagues sufficient opportunity to answer questions and share their complete thoughts. Americans are very comfortable speaking over each other. Europeans generally don't operate that way and can be put off when Americans do.
- If you're looking to blend in, one easy, superficial way to do this is to listen to the tone of your voice. American accents stand out in Europe and sound relatively indelicate to European ears. The lilts and notes we hit when we talk simply aren't the same. How we ask questions is the most obvious example. Brits ask questions in a singsong way that ends on a higher note. Americans ask questions in a more monotone way that sounds less like a question to a Brit—it sounds more like a command. You may not choose to change your accent, but you'll want to make sure your polite intentions are understood as such.
- Remember that cheerleading is a particularly American phenomenom. The American style of leadership often comes with a great deal of overt energy and enthusiasm, but many countries don't have the same rah-rah culture. As a result, colleagues outside of America sometimes don't believe the sincerity of an eagerly offered congratulations or thank-you.

> • Ultimately, if you're working abroad, how much you want to assimilate to your host country's culture is your own personal choice. The good news is that acknowledging and celebrating our differences is often fertile ground for relationship building.

What's the lesson? Be sensitive to others' communication methods. Make the effort to head off miscommunications as early as possible. Evaluate which employees speak more emotionally and let them know when they need to temper their speech. Identify which employees won't understand your sarcasm or dry sense of humor. And, perhaps most importantly, don't punish people for their style of communication, although some things, such as abusive swearing, are never acceptable and always unprofessional. Generally, though, it's just a style difference and it's your job to get everybody on the same page.

a look through johari's window

Wading through the management teachings, we occasionally stumble on some "theory" that seems interesting enough to break down and share.

The Johari Window is a tool that management consultants use to help increase communication within organizations. It was created by Joe Luft and Harry Ingham at the University of California in the 1950s. Their window offers a way of looking at how communication is expressed. Simply put, the window reflects the interaction of information between self and others. Good communication happens in the top left quadrant, known as the "arena," the area that is "known by self" and "known by others." Below the "arena" is the "facade," the quadrant where you know but others don't. The quad-

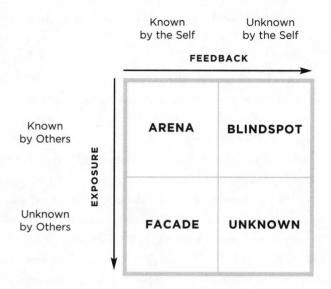

Known by the Self | Unknown by the Self

FEEDBACK

EXPOSURE

Known by Others

| ARENA | BLINDSPOT |

Unknown by Others

| FACADE | UNKNOWN |

rant next to the "arena" is the "blindspot," where others know but you don't. And below the "blindspot" is the "unknown," the quadrant where neither you nor others know.

Their assumption is that productivity and interpersonal effectiveness are directly related to the amount of information that is shared between you and others. For example, if a manager knows that a member of her team has just relocated from another country, and the team member knows that communication is different in their new country, then chances are they will work together to try to understand each other before jumping to conclusions.

Your goal (without sharing unnecessary personal information, of course) is to make the arena as large as possible. The larger the arena becomes, the more rewarding, effective, and productive the relationship can be. You can increase the size of the arena by regular and honest exchange of feedback and a willingness to disclose personal feelings. People around you will understand what "makes you tick," and what you find easy or difficult to do, and can provide appropriate support. And, of course, you can then do the same for them.

INCREASING THE SIZE OF THE ARENA

Influencing the size of the arena is in your control. The more you share relevant information you have with others, the more you enlarge the arena in a downward direction, reducing the facade. Luft and Ingham call this the "exposure" process, and it requires open and candid expression of feelings and facts.

It takes two to communicate, and the other party must also expose (share information) in order for communication to be productive. Therefore, you must actively solicit information from others. Luft and Ingham call this "feedback solicitation." As you receive feedback, the arena extends to the right, reducing your blindspot.

To establish effective communication, you need to engage in exposure and feedback soliciting—give information and ask questions of others. It's all in your control, and as the manager, it's your responsibility to increase the arena. When Sarilee Norton was a vice president at Tenneco Packaging, she would schedule a quarterly meeting to review goals and objectives. She told us, "Getting people to use their brains—intellect, creativity, sensitivity—and at the same time drawing them in on a personal level can really have an impact. I used to do a quarterly lunch and ask each participant to do something that would give the group insight into the individual and what motivated them. For example, one lunch I asked each person to bring an object from their past that would reveal something we probably didn't know about them. Barb, my executive assistant, brought her toe shoes and clippings from when she danced semiprofessionally. None of us knew she was a dancer. Diana brought Boo-boo, her childhood teddy bear, which she packed in her overnight bag whenever she traveled because it brought her back to earth even on a bad day. Then each person would talk about the projects they were working on, what was going well and what wasn't, where they needed help or maybe some input from the others. Finally, we'd review our objectives and initiatives for the period and assess how we thought we were doing." The exposing of personal information and giving others insight into one another's personalities made the group closer and therefore facilitated more positive communication.

girl talk

GRETCHEN MONAHAN: GRETTACOLE, G SPA, GRETTA LUXE

Gretchen "Gretta" Monahan is building a small empire of salons, day spas, and fashion boutiques in the Boston area and appears regularly as a makeover coach on TLC's *A Makeover Story*. Gretchen took out a loan in 1995 to start Grettacole (www.gretta cole.com), and today she has approximately 110 employees and six businesses, including three Grettacole full-service salons and day spas, two Gretta Luxe fashion boutiques, and the newest brand, G Spa, which provides "quickie" spa services. Gretchen also offers women personalized online consultations with tips on hair, makeup, skin treatment, and clothing.

In 2000, Gretchen was one of Boston's premier stylists and the "star" and owner of her flagship salon, Grettacole, in Wellesley, Massachusetts. She worked eighty hours a week "doing heads" and training and managing a team of stylists. When she opened her second store, she simply split her eighty-hour week into two forties, one in each store. As the stores became more and more successful, others soon followed. She began to believe that her dream of launching a national style brand could be attained, but things would have to change.

First, she would have to pull herself out of the salon, stop doing hair, and become a leader for the team: a spokesperson for the company and an executive with a grasp of the financials and a vision for the future—a pretty tall order for a hairstylist without even a college degree. So Gretchen sought out the support she needed to achieve her goals. Based on the advice of a mentor, she applied for and won admittance to the prestigious entrepreneur's MBA program at the Harvard Business School. We talked to Gretchen about her corporate culture and management style.

How would you describe your corporate culture?

We have a very high-touch business, are full of aspiration, and focus on client care. We don't push paperwork and aren't overly reliant on systems, although as we continue to grow this will change, too. The challenge is that change in salon culture takes years to achieve. We've been successful so far because we've proven that if a stylist follows our program and stays true to our core values of allover client care, happiness, and satisfaction, then they will be more successful than in other salons and make more money.

How is your business organized?

Each business unit has a salaried manager who is responsible for the success of that business and all of the people who work in it. At Grettacole, we don't just do hair. We offer an integrated beauty and fashion experience, and because it is unique, both the team members and clients need to be educated. I try to run the organization as a family, as most of the senior management team has been with me since the beginning and has helped me develop the values and systems that have made us successful.

How do you communicate your vision and culture to your employees?

In the beginning I led completely by example. I touched everyone. I trained every new member of the team and met all of the clients, making sure each client's needs were met and that everyone on the team, from the receptionist on up, offered our clients "the Grettacole experience." I realized that this "star" system was not scaleable, and I had to find a way to communicate the Grettacole values to 110 employees in six stores as well as the hundreds of clients in a very different way.

I had to abort mission on the star system and pretty darn quick. I offered my core team the opportunity to become leaders. I asked them to put aside their fears of abandonment and encouraged them to take a leadership role and climb up the corporate ladder with me because there's a lot of room at the top. But more importantly, I had to convince them that there was value in the organization without the star and building the brand. They had to trust the training that I had given them for years and seize the opportunity to grow. As more time passed without me in the salon, they realized that they could continue the standards that we developed together. As the president and spokesperson, I can monitor, support, teach, and demonstrate, but I can't hold anyone's hands anymore.

How have things changed for you and the business?
I'm proud to say the business continues to grow and prosper. The most drastic change has been in how we communicate with one another. I had always worked face to face, chair to chair if you will, so switching to a predominantly e-mail and phone call communication was a huge change. We're now dependent on the computer managing our calendars, and communication with long-term senior members of staff is almost strictly by e-mail. I was in Milan viewing the collections for Grettaluxe when I got an e-mail from my assistant telling me that one of the original members of my team, Julie Deane, was going to be out of work because her son was diagnosed with cancer. Wow, I thought, and I am getting this horrible news in the middle of the night on my BlackBerry. I wrote right back letting them know how sorry I was and that I could be home tomorrow if she needed me to fill in. The hard facts are that there are no balances in life, only trade-offs. I wasn't there in person for my friend. I spoke to her on the phone and she told me to stay and work, they were okay and she would check in with me via e-mail. Fortunately, her son has made an incredible recovery. What I realized is that in actual fact, I hadn't been communicating with her in person for some time. At Grettacole, we never interrupt a stylist when they are with a client, so when I call the store, Julie rarely has time to come to the phone. We always e-mail about work issues, and now we began e-mailing about personal issues.

Tragically, a few days later, my mother died unexpectedly in her sleep. And Julie was there for me, with e-mails and phone calls and support. I'm very lucky. I started the company. I want the company to grow. I signed up for the long hours and the sacrifices, but only because of the accomplishments and skill of the team around me am I able to achieve my goals and dreams. I try to always remember that. What I realized during the hard times is that life is precious, and people are what matter. Sure, I will continue to work hard and accomplish my goals, but I will never trade in my relationships. I've seen too many CEOs or people on television begin to drink their own bath water. They create their own "star system," and forget that their most valuable assets are their employees. The reality is that it is so much easier to go and do hair. You get instant, gratifying feedback from the clients, you can make lots of money, and your only concern is yourself. But that's not building a business, a business that can provide for the well-being of many other people. My dream is that the discipline I now demonstrate will pay off for everybody in the future, and the enterprise will be a sustainable, high-quality, high-integrity brand that we will all be proud to be a part of for years to come.

office politics are a big fat drag

NAVIGATING CLOSED DOORS, HUSHED WHISPERS, AND WATERCOOLER RUMORS

We know. We thought we left this behavior behind in high school. We assumed we'd grown up and moved on from the backstabbing and gossip, but as we all know, those passed notes and ruined reputations were just a dress rehearsal for the big show.

Glamour magazine joined with www.lawyers.com to conduct a poll that revealed that 75 percent of women say we're tougher on other females than we are on men in the workplace. Of all the social institutions we graduate into, the workplace can be the worst kind of incubator for mean-spirited, ugly, and jealous behavior, all of which culminates in the lowest form of politics.

It shouldn't be this way, and women managers can change the tone and culture in today's workplace. The era of the old boys' club is coming to an end. According to the Center for Women's Business Research, 28 percent of women now earn more than their husbands.

And women today represent 50 percent of the graduating classes in law schools, medical schools, and MBA programs.

In 2000, CNN executive Gail Evans wrote a groundbreaking, bestselling book, *Play Like a Man, Win Like a Woman: What Men Know About Success that Women Need to Learn*. In *Play Like a Man, Win Like a Woman*, Evans put forth her thesis: Women are not in star positions because they haven't yet learned how to play the game. She believed that the game of business is played on a field where males have been comfortable since they were very young. Evans wrote, "It's a game where winning is the obvious (and only) objective and where aggression, self-promotion, a tough skin, and an effective display of power are the signs of a winner. Women, on the other hand, enter the game disadvantaged, having been taught to be cooperative rather than competitive, to enjoy the process rather than simply the result, and to seek approval rather than assume success." In her book, Evans sets out to level the playing field by instructing women on how men play so that we can beat them at their own game.

Three short years later, Evans wrote a second bestselling book, *She Wins, You Win: The Most Important Strategies for Making Women More Powerful*, where she advises women to trump the old boys' network by playing a "girls' game." She realized that it's not about playing games like men. It's about winning as women, and doing it together. Her rule in this book: "Every time a woman succeeds in business, every other woman's chance of succeeding in business increases. Every time a woman fails in business, every other woman's chance of failure increases."

As Gail Evans's flip-flop demonstrates, in a very short time women's power and sheer numbers have changed the rules in the workplace, but make no mistake, the game is still on. And you had better know the rules. Playing politics takes time and energy away from accomplishing your goals and undermines the efforts of both you and your team, but sometimes you just can't avoid the game.

the world outside your office door: what office politics are and why they suck

Personality clashes. Interdepartmental competition. Sucking up to the boss. Gossiping. Acting one way with your team and another way with your management. These are just a few examples of office politics. According to the career-planning section of www.about.com, office politics is an increasing problem, as evidenced by a 1998 study from Accountemps published in *Talent Scout*: "Eighteen percent of an administrator's time—more than nine weeks out of every year—is spent resolving conflicts among employees."

Managers and employees who are spending more time playing politics are spending less time on their jobs—impacting productivity and eventually the bottom line. Politics isn't just a big-company phenomenon. We've interviewed a number of people who worked in retail and restaurants (not to mention all of the postings we've seen on career advice Web sites and job complaint blogs) who've complained that the staff members who were "most friendly" with the bosses got the best shifts and schedules. "Bosses' pets" were held to a different standard than the other employees, and this created problems. It's impossible not to like some people more than others, but as a manager, your responsibility is to make sure that your team has the tools and the environment to get their work accomplished.

Terry Bragg runs a company called Peacemakers Training in Salt Lake City and works with organizations to create a workplace where people want to work, and with managers who want their people to work together better. In a 2004 article for *Occupational Hazards* magazine, he offered "Nine Strategies for Successfully Playing Office Politics":

1. Be nice to everyone. Don't believe the "nice guys finish last" stuff. In office politics, nice guys build supportive relationships with other people. Bulldozers and sharks make enemies, and enemies make your life miserable by resisting and sabotaging you. Be sincerely nice to everyone, not just the people you think can help you. People resent phoniness.

2. Be a team player. A team player is someone who helps the team achieve its goals and helps other people achieve their goals. Be a star by making other people look good, rather than taking credit for other people's achievements.

3. Don't whine and complain. Develop a reputation for being a problem solver. Anybody can complain about a problem, but really valuable employees are those who prevent or solve problems. Although the squeaky wheel may get oiled, its coworkers resent the whiny employee.

4. Be visible. You can't win office politics by hiding. You must be involved and others need to perceive you as a valuable contributor at work. Get involved in solving important and highly visible problems at work. In the age of downsizing, many employees are shocked to learn that they lost their jobs because upper management didn't know what they were contributing to their organization. You not only have to do good work; others must give you credit for your good work and perceive you as a good worker.

5. Help your boss succeed. This is part of being a team player. It is also a smart strategy because your boss is a major player in your promotability and in how upper management perceives you and your work. If you have a positive relationship with your boss, your boss is more likely to support your career and help you advance. Now some of you are reeling in disgust because you hate your boss.

Well, get over it. You will have a more difficult time winning office politics if you openly declare war on your boss or antagonize your boss. Remember, he probably has kept his job and power base because he knows a few things about playing office politics. You don't have to suck up to your boss, but you must nurture your relationship with your boss. If you disagree with your boss, do it privately. Be very careful about embarrassing your boss in public or in front of your boss's superiors or staff. You don't want your boss trying to get even with you.

6. Be loyal. Avoid backbiting and backstabbing. Coworkers will support you if they believe that you will be there to support them. To get loyalty, show your loyalty.

7. Be good at what you do. Develop your expertise and competence. Show up on time and work hard for your full shift. To survive in the workplace, you need to do good work. If others perceive you as a slacker or a poor worker, they will not support you. They will also resent your getting promoted before them.

8. Mind your manners. Be polite and courteous. Avoid being sarcastic or putting other people down. Err on the side of being gracious.

9. Make other people look good. We already mentioned this concerning being a team player, but it bears repeating. People will support you when they believe that you make them look good. They will resent you if they believe you take credit for the work they do. Give credit to others. Sincerely compliment others. Help people look important and successful in front of the people who are important to them.

good witch or big bitch?

IT'S NOT ALWAYS FAIR: SOME BITCHES GET TO THE TOP
Jane and Sarah are two of the most kick-ass saleswomen in Chicago working for one of the hottest companies in the industry. They regularly exceed their sales goals and are loved by customers and other departments alike. Unfortunately, they are miserable and with good reason. They work for a big bitch boss—a boss who routinely breaks every rule in this book.

- She routinely eavesdrops on their conversations and berates them about the content. God forbid they are on a personal call, she will walk out of her office and into theirs, standing in front of them tapping her foot until they hang up.
- She requires Jane and Sarah to blind-copy her on all e-mails with outside customers so she knows exactly what they are saying. It's distrustful and disrespectful, and makes them second guess everything they say.
- She screams. Regularly and for no apparent reason.
- She takes credit for their accomplishments with senior management, and often with them in a meeting bearing witness.
- She places blame when things go wrong and never accepts responsibility.
- She is absolutely out of control when it comes to budgeting and managing costs, without ever considering the big picture. She will regularly fly off the handle if a budget line needs to be increased, even if another line is reduced to cancel out the overage.
- She will override their opinion in front of customers, their assistants, outside consultants, messengers, pretty much anyone in the universe, other than her own management, of course.
- Two excellent (reliable, smart, and friendly) department assistants sit outside Jane and Sarah's supervisor's office. She

doesn't like their phone manner, they are much too friendly. She e-mails Jane and Sarah to ask them to be less friendly on the phone. "They don't need to be so sweet, it wastes time."

Jane and Sarah's supervisor was recently promoted and given more responsibility. In addition to all of those things they listed above, their manager is a master of politics. She has an uncanny knack for survival and has put her own needs and goals above all else, and so far it's been working for her. Her management has chosen to look the other way because the department continues to produce. We believe her bad boss behavior will catch up with her. We just hope it's soon enough for Jane and Sarah.

girl's guide to gossip

In this book, we've interviewed experts about each subject we cover. We've included real-life stories from ourselves and others. Kim is the world's living expert on workplace gossip—she's excelled at it, been burned by it, used it to her advantage, and almost been fired for it on a few occasions early in her career. She was never a malicious gossip, but she has the gift. She remembers people, faces, and places and has an uncanny ability to put the pieces of a story together even when nobody tells her anything. She can listen and participate in a number of different conversations at the same time, and as an operator in the days before voice-mail, she would routinely answer the phones of thirty different people, getting to know each of their stories: who their friends and lovers were, what they liked for lunch, when they went to hair or personal fitness appointments, who their shrink was, and on and on. She was friendly and chatty and occasionally passed along inappropriate information. Now she's a repentant gossip and here's her hard-learned Girl's Guide to Workplace Gossip:

- Keep it to yourself. It's not easy, but when you learn a new piece of information, don't share it with anyone.
- Satisfy the urge with celebrities. Our favorite way to blow off steam and share gossip is to talk about celebrities—let's face it, their stories are always more exciting than your coworkers' or bosses' will ever be.
- Set some boundaries and stick to them. You don't need to share every detail of your personal life. If you don't know what we're talking about, review chapter 4's section on setting boundaries.
- Sharing positive news doesn't give you a free pass. Remember, it is not your story to tell. If a member of your team or your boss tells you they are pregnant, it is not information for you to pass along.
- If someone tells you something, assume that they don't want you to tell someone else.
- Being trustworthy can be your biggest asset. If you are a trusted member of an organization, you will be given more responsibility, more information, and more power.
- Don't ever use names in public. For this one we have to credit Caitlin's husband, Andrew. You just never know who you're sitting next to in a restaurant, on an airplane, or at your child's soccer game.
- Information is currency, but you don't have to treat it that way.
- If you overhear some information, don't pass it along. Remember, it may not even be true.
- Avoid negative talk. Complaining doesn't make things better and it usually makes it worse.
- If you have an idea how to improve something, share it. Creating positive buzz can be very beneficial to an organization.
- If you do plan on passing something along, whatever you do, do not write it down (no e-mail!). Ever. Pick up the phone. We try not to subscribe to the "CYA" manual; however, in this case we

must. When you write something down, there is no denying that you said it. Written words and e-mails can be passed along and can never be denied. Trust us. Cover your ass by not committing gossip to paper.

- If your role in the company puts you in contact with confidential personnel or financial information, keep it to yourself. For so many reasons. You can hurt people and the company, and you will be fired for breaking confidentiality.

don't date: it's the law

We find that women fall into two camps when it comes to workplace dating: those who do and those who don't. Our Marines from chapter 2 were a good example. Courtney had a policy against dating Marines; Angela dated a Marine (not in her chain of command) and wound up marrying him. Caitlin was an office dater. As a matter of fact, she too married her boss from a previous job. However, if she were to do it all over again, she probably would try to avoid workplace dating. Not only did she have to find another job to continue her relationship; when her team found out, she became an instant pariah. Being a pariah is bad, but being the subject of a lawsuit is certainly worse.

In a ruling that significantly expands the law on sexual harassment in the workplace in 2005, California's Supreme Court ruled that workers can sue when a colleague who is sleeping with the boss is shown repeated preferential treatment.

According to the *New York Times*, "Unions and lawyers who represent workers rejoiced, claiming a victory for a group some of them call 'the unloved.' Phil Horowitz, chairman of the California Employment Lawyers Association, said employees can no longer be 'treated as second-class citizens because they're not putting out.' "

Lawmakers in other states are looking at this ruling and considering recommending similar legislation. Think twice before dating a colleague, and it's probably better to just avoid dating the boss, especially if he's married. You'd think this is common sense, yet it happens all of the time. It's also important to remember that society's acceptance of women dating in the workplace or cheating on their husbands is a lot lower. If a woman is going to try to date the boss, she had better be sure that it's going to be worth it. Suzy Wetlaufer may have gotten former CEO Jack Welch to leave his wife and marry her, but she also lost her job and had to weather being trashed in the newspapers and on television for months.

So, you've ruled out workplace dating. You should probably rule out joking, too. When we asked our house counsel, employment attorney Laurie Malkin, how dangerous it is to even joke about sex, she gave us the long and frightening answer:

"It is *incredibly* dangerous. A workplace that includes sexual jokes can be a 'hostile environment' under federal, state, and local laws that prohibit sexual harassment. Although a single instance of a sexually related joke or innuendo does not, in itself, make an employer liable for sexual harassment, an environment that condones such conduct—particularly one in which managers or supervisors engage in such behavior—is begging for trouble.

"Women can be held liable for sexual harassment just as easily as men. Both women and men also can be held liable for same-sex harassment, so telling jokes among the 'girls' also may give rise to legal liability. Supervisors and corporate officers may, in many cases, be held *personally liable* for unlawful harassment and discrimination. This means that a plaintiff may be able to go after a person's own bank accounts, home, personal property, future wages, etc., if he or she prevails and wins money damages. Finally, keep in mind that even if a female manager wins the legal battle, she may have lost the war—few employers stand by their employees when they are found to have engaged in improper or illegal conduct. It also does little to help one's image and business relationships.

"The above warnings are not idle threats. The average jury verdict in a sexual harassment case is $250,000, not including legal fees, court costs, and punitive damages. These additional amounts can more than double the cost. The U.S. Equal Employment Opportunity Commission, the agency that administers federal antidiscrimination laws, reports that allegations of sexual harassment *by men* is up dramatically—from 9.1 percent of all claims in 1992 to 15.1 percent in 2004. Add these two facts together, mix with old-fashioned greed and a national culture that loves a good scandal, and you have a recipe for disaster.

MANAGING YOUR MANAGER

As an employee, when faced with highly political environment, you can do a few things to make life easier for yourself and with your supervisor. A number of the managers, when sharing their experiences, unknowingly shared their frustrations about their staff. Like communication, frustration is a two-way street. We've culled all of the frustrations, threw in our own, and came up with a list of things to help you be a better employee. If you honor your end of the bargain, we can guarantee you will be better managed.

- It's not about you. You are not the most important cog in the wheel and should not be the focus of everyone's attention. Consider your role and try to look at your manager's challenges in addition to your own.
- Get to know your boss's challenges and help solve them. If you become known as a problem-solver, your boss will give you more responsibility and better assignments, and quicker promotion.
- Make yourself useful. If you see something that needs to be

done, do it. An "It's Not My Job" attitude gets you nowhere with your management.

- Know your boss's schedule and try to work within it. For example, if you know that she has a weekly meeting with her management on a certain day, then communicate your accomplishments and challenges to her the day before.
- Be loyal. If your manager has treated you fairly and with support, you owe her some allegiance.
- A little initiative goes a long way. Every single manager we interviewed said they preferred employees who took chances and made mistakes to those who waited and regularly asked for instruction.
- Know the pecking order. If you're a new employee, chances are you're at the bottom of it. Don't worry, we've all been there.
- If you're unhappy, speak up. Be specific about the problems you're having and try to come to the conversation with some solutions.

the high road less traveled

It's pretty boring, and it's never easy. However, the best advice we can offer you to be successful in office politics is to just take the high road. If everyone around you is being negative, keep your mouth shut. If someone shares a juicy piece of gossip with you, don't pass it along. If the office hours are flexible, and most people show up late, get in on time. Maintain friendly relationships with everyone, even if you can't stand them.

the word

ELIZABETH SPIERS, NOVELIST AND FORMER
EDITOR IN CHIEF, MEDIABISTRO.COM

As founding editor of Gawker.com, a weblog about "the darker Manhattan-centric themes: class warfare as recreational sport; pathological status obsession; and the complete, total, and wholly unapologetic embrace of decadence," she became a celeb herself. She was named one of *Women's Wear Daily*'s "Ones to Watch" in October of 2004 and "Best Gossip" by the *Village Voice* ("Best of New York") in 2003. Gawker was named to *Entertainment Weekly*'s 2003 "IT List," one of *Time* magazine's "Top 50 Websites" for 2003, a "Best Media Blog" (2003) by *Forbes*, and a "Best of Breed" online news site by the New York New Media Association.

Elizabeth was the editor in chief of mediabistro.com, a Web site whose mission is to "provide opportunities (both on- and offline) for you to meet each other, share resources, become informed of job opportunities and interesting projects, improve your career skills, and showcase your work." She's also been a contributing writer and editor at *New York* magazine and a freelance writer for a number of publications, and her résumé even includes a stint as a buy-side financial analyst focusing on small-cap tech equities and early-stage venture capital. She's currently writing a novel. She's been at the forefront of new media, worked in traditional media, and even did a stint on Wall Street. Elizabeth shares some thoughts on blogging and office politics with us:

- People risk losing their jobs for blogging about work for the same reason people write about work generally: It takes up half of your waking life. It's hard not to write about work. People who do it in such a way that it might jeopardize their jobs are usually just telling themselves that it's not a big deal or their boss won't find it.

- Perhaps because I've generally been good with office politics, I don't think they're a "problem" to be solved. There are hierarchies in every aspect of life, and they're not going to go away, so best learn how to navigate them. Different kinds of workplaces have different kinds of problems. The things that made my life difficult when I was an equity analyst are not the same things that make my life difficult in the media industry.

- Working for Gawker was essentially the same as freelance writing. You're working from home and no one's really telling you what to do. Working in traditional media at *New York* magazine (though to be fair, I was also blogging for them) was like having a nine-to-five desk job, except that, being a magazine, it was less rigorous bureaucratically than, say, a consulting or finance job. It's a creative pursuit and much more easygoing, professionally. I actually liked the magazine environment better because being around other people was more stimulating than sitting on my couch all day with a laptop. There were other people I could learn from. Mediabistro is a job that's environmentally more like a dot-com, but my particular job is more similar to the magazine job than the Gawker job. I'm in the office all day, managing other people, assigning and editing stories, etc.

- The friend/editor boundaries are loose in my experience. I get together socially with many of my editors, past and present, and several of my bloggers and freelance writers have also become personal friends. You just have to be rigorous about setting boundaries, and if there's any sort of conflict you have to make sure they understand that you're doing your best to be sympathetic (and are probably more inclined to be, given your personal relationship), but you have your own job requirements. In situations where the personal relationship predates your professional relationship, the general rule of thumb should be don't hire your friends unless you're capable of firing them, should that become necessary.

go ahead and blog: you may just get fired for it

We've established that you can be fired for dating your boss and coming in late. That seems pretty obvious compared to the new craze in fire-able offenses: blogging about your workplace. Only a few will be able to turn their blogs into six-figure book deals and movie options. So most likely, what worked for Jessica Cutler, author of *The Washingtonienne* and famous blogger who got fired from the mail room in the office of Senator Mike DeWine after sharing her experiences trading sex for money with high-profile Washington politicos, will not work for you. As she herself said when interviewed in the *Washington Post* when the scandal broke, "I was only blogging for, what, less than two weeks? Some people with blogs are never going to get famous, and they've been doing it for, like, over a year. I feel bad for them."

For those of you who are not blogging about being paid for sex by politicians but merely complaining that your boss and coworkers are lazy and irritating, take heed. You can and probably will be fired if someone from your workplace reads it. According to an article in *USA Today* in 2005, "Delta Air Lines, Google and other major companies are firing and disciplining employees for what they say about work on their blogs, which are personal sites that often contain a mix of frank commentary, freewheeling opinions and journaling."

Blogs are everywhere. According to a report this year by public relations firm Edelman and Intelliseek, a provider of business-intelligence solutions, about twenty thousand new blogs are created daily, and an estimated 10 million U.S. blogs will exist by the end of 2005. Together, these blogs link up to create what is known as a blogosphere, a collective Internet conversation that is one of the fastest-growing areas of new content on the Web.

Workplace blogging can be scary territory. Employees who create blogs set up a direct way to communicate about their company with the public, because customers and clients can stumble across a blog when doing a seemingly harmless Google search. And isn't that kind of the point? You're not blogging for yourself—that could be done on the private hard drive of your computer—you're blogging so other people will read it. And if other people read about incompetence in your workplace, interoffice affairs, or new projects that you're working on, you can put your employer and yourself at risk.

Because blogging is so new, laws haven't been written concerning it yet and companies are just beginning to write their policies.

We recommend using common sense when blogging.

- Don't complain, slander, or otherwise disrespect people who you work with.
- Don't blog about your sex life, or your drinking habits, or recreational drug use. Many employers have "morals clauses," and if you break them, even on your personal time, you will be fired.
- Don't assume you're anonymous. The more salacious your blog, the more people who read will try and figure out who you are.
- Don't blog about the projects you are working on—this could be considered privileged information by your employer.

Of course, if you can't blog about any of the above, then there may be no reason to blog at all—which is the safest route.

girl talk

FRANKE JAMES

Franke James describes herself as an artist/inventor/writer and a founder of www.office-politics.com. She has been developing new creative products, everything from games to cartoons, since 1997. She's designed lighthearted "psychological" and satirical Internet games. The office-politics site was conceived in 2000 as a place that people could turn to for information, advice, and entertainment about all things office politics. People love the free advice column, and she's received thousands of posts from all over the world and from all kinds of industries. To handle the volume, she's assembled a growing list of authors, executive coaches, and ethical experts. Her latest project is the Office-Politics® game. Franke shares her experiences with office politics with us.

What is the most common dilemma you hear?
Nobody appreciates all the work I do.

In the Office-Politics® game many of the situations you present are much more serious than office politics. You cover harassment and petty white-collar crime and a number of basic ethical situations. What parameters should be put on office politics vs. more serious offenses?
Office politics is about the ethical culture and values that everyone in the office shares (or doesn't share!). So, you have to ask yourself, What are the important values in my office? Do I fit in? Are openness and honesty encouraged, or are lying, cheating, and bribery the unspoken rule? Depending on who you are and what your values are, you are going to be a fish out of water in one office and swimming happily in the other. Obviously most offices are not that black and white; there is a huge scale, but it's the old slippery slope. Is lying okay when it's the executive secretary covering for the boss? Is lying okay when safety inspectors come to investigate a contamination problem because otherwise it will cause

mayhem with the stock price? Is paying bribes okay because that's the way business is run in this country? It goes on and on.

I see office politics as encompassing all ethical, behavioral, and moral issues encountered in the office environment. It's about human nature. Family politics and school politics share many of the same dynamics.

Can you succeed in business without playing politics? If so, do you have any suggestions for women to minimize the political landscape?

You can't escape office politics. But you can learn to play the game. Everyone has an agenda. Awareness makes all the difference. It's much better to understand how and why people are manipulating facts and/or events to bring about their desired outcome. Office politics are not a necessarily evil. They are a fact of life and everyone is better off learning how to deal with them—and how to use them to their advantage!

People need to be asking themselves questions all the time, such as, How do my needs differ from the company's needs? How are they in sync? How can achieving my career objectives benefit the company? Who do I need to sell my idea to within the company to make positive change happen? Whose agenda will block my idea? etc.

How bad does a situation have to get before you bring it to the attention of your supervisor or human resources?

Use your best judgment. Obviously if it's a petty matter (e.g., who got the better chair, better vacation dates, etc.), then you want to rise above it so you aren't branded as petty and small-minded.

But if it's illegal, or harassment—sexual or psychological—don't wait. Life is too short, and the price of stress too high to put up with a problem that's gnawing away at you or a coworker.

What are you three absolute "must never dos" in the workplace for women?

1. *Don't bitch about petty things.* Choose your battles so you
don't come off looking like squabbling children. Many bosses

abdicate responsibility in deciding who is right and who is wrong. They are frequently impatient, and just as likely to fire the innocent as the guilty.

2. *Don't do anything you wouldn't want to see splashed across the front page of the newspaper.* It's old advice, but good, especially in this age of camera cell phones! Would Enron and Worldcom have had their respective meltdowns if the company culture was zero tolerance for dishonesty?

3. *Don't mix office and romance.* This is a tough one for many people. After all, we see our coworkers for more hours in the week than our spouses. If you do succumb to temptation, have a good exit plan.

Are there strategies to adopt as managers to stop the politics before they can start?

Managers should hire for attitude, not ability. You can train someone to learn a new skill, but it's awfully hard to change ingrained attitudes (hmmm, brainwashing might work, but it's iffy). Attitudes set the stage for the company culture. The manager's hires should reflect the ideal company culture. This helps create one big, happy family where people generally embrace the same values, honesty, truthfulness, diligence vs. lying, cheating, etc. That is true whether it's a good culture or a bad culture you want to build.

being the boss without being bossy

BUSINESS LESSONS YOU LEARNED IN CHILDHOOD

Believe it or not, most people learn all they need to know about being the boss by the time they are five. Unfortunately, those basic principles that are written in stone while under the watchful eyes of our mothers, fathers, and teachers are all but lost once we are thrust out into the real world. But these forgotten nuggets are great tips for making it as an adult in the wonderful world of work.

Remember too-tall Tina, who threatened you every day during recess? She might have gotten your lunch money, but she never earned your respect. Think back to the little boy who copied off your paper in study hall. Well, he might have gotten an A in English, but we heard he got busted last year for insider trading. And that little tattletale who told on you for passing notes in class? Well sure, he is a hugely successful judge, but everyone hates him!

sharing is caring

You didn't meet your sales goals, win the account, or take the company public alone, did you? On a daily basis, the individuals on your team bring their unique talents to the table and work together to accomplish professional goals. Yes, you guide the staff by making the plan, answering the questions, and settling the disputes. But they are still working, contributing, and creating on behalf of the company and you will not inspire them to do any of it well if you treat them as just cogs in your wheel. It takes a confident manager to step aside and give credit where credit is due. Nothing will inspire loyalty like a boss who acknowledges that she didn't do it flying solo.

Along with sharing credit, effective managers need to also share information. If you are busy, it is easier to deliver pieces of only the most time-sensitive information. But you are doing your team a disservice by not sharing the whole picture. When delegating a project, tell your team how it fits into the company's goals. If your CEO has decided to launch a new identity campaign or new product, then tell your staff about it. If there is a bad review coming out for the restaurant you manage, make sure to tell the waitstaff. Information helps your team do a better job in both the short run (day-to-day tasks) and the long run (professional goal-setting). It helps them plan, grow, and think big picture.

she did it!

If the team makes a serious mistake, then the good boss takes the blame. That is the way it should be. Your power and salary are higher than everyone below you on the corporate ladder for a reason. It really is your ass, and possibly your job, on the line when a project goes wrong. Eating crow can be frustrating when it was your assistant who forgot to overnight the presentation, but that goes with the territory. Imagine what your boss would think of you if, when criticized for something, you pointed at your fresh-faced assistant and said "She did it!" When helping her boss with an event, Ilene Kramer, an assistant to a high-profile event planner, mistakenly ordered five hundred, not five thousand, invitations. When she found out, her boss said it was a huge mistake but worked with her to fix it. When the client called, she let her scream, sucked it up, and apologized on behalf of the company. Because she had protected her employee and partnered with her to solve the problem, she earned her respect and, more importantly, her loyalty. It takes self-confidence to take a bullet for the team, but have faith that by taking responsibility, your boss and direct reports will respect you for it.

the word

AMY COSTELLO, KINDERGARTEN TEACHER

Amy Costello is a kindergarten teacher and a mother of two. We spoke to her about what she tries to teach the kids under her care and were shocked by how applicable it all was to the workplace. We think Amy would make an amazing corporate mentor and manager.

- If Jimmy did something that bothered Rachel, then I encourage her not to talk to other people about it and not to dwell on it but rather to bring it up directly with him. I find that children will immediately come to me or talk to their friends when something has hurt them, but rarely is the first person they talk to the instigator.
- I teach kids to be organized. I work with them to create a

place for everything such as homework, jacket, hats, and mittens. Everything we do at this stage is about setting up good habits.

- We want the children to learn to take responsibility for themselves, their work, and the impact they have on the world around them. The buck stops with them, so if they lose their homework, it isn't okay to say "my mom forgot."

- I think it is really important that all of the kids have a goal to work on. At the beginning of the school year I sit down with each of them and set a goal. For one it could be learning to tie their shoes, for another it could be learning to read additional words. It helps keep them focused on something, and the sense of accomplishment they have when the goal is achieved is a wonderful thing for their self-esteem.

- They have to learn to be on time. We don't want anyone to think it is okay to be late to their desks, groups, or classes, so we teach them to look at the clock.

- I try to teach them that a positive attitude is everything. We play a little game and for a day they go about their lives seeing if their smile will get a smile back. When they realize that almost everyone they encounter smiles back, they understand how impactful their attitude is on the people around them.

- We want all of them to understand that we are all different and that everyone has strengths. We encourage the children to work together to make the most of these strengths. If Jonathan is having a hard time with writing his A's, we set him up with Jennifer, who has great handwriting. If Jennifer is having a hard time organizing her cubby, then we ask Ethan to give her a hand because he is very neat.

- We teach them to take pride in their work by having them do it over if it is sloppy, or if I know they can do better.

- The only mistake they can make with me is not trying.

don't be a know-it-all

Yes, chances are good that you know the answer and the best way to do things. And yes, your ideas are most likely smarter than the ones that your team comes up with. But so what? That is why they pay you the big bucks. To empower your people, you need to listen and make them feel heard. In brainstorms get their ideas, in meetings ask their opinions, and in reviews respect their point of view. If you have gathered a diverse, intelligent group of people to support you, then their contributions are only going to add to a proposal, presentation, or new product development. Keep in mind, if you do solicit ideas, then occasionally you need to implement them. Donna Lynn, a nurse at a city hospital, told us her supervisor asks everyone for their ideas on how to tweak management and improve schedules every month. After a few months of stuffing the "idea box" with what they thought were excellent suggestions and noticing that literally not one was implemented, the nurses gave up. "It became quickly obvious that they were just playing at management, trying out something they had read in some book. They didn't really care about us or our ideas." Don't just pay lip service; your team will catch on quickly.

one face is better than two

So your boss is an ineffectual, unlikable bitch and you would like nothing better than to share that with everyone you meet. Just because you would like to, doesn't mean that you should. If you don't like your boss, then work on changing how she treats you or quit. Those are your only options. Being negative by complaining about her to your staff sets a bad precedent. You are demonstrating to them that it is acceptable to be disrespectful, and complaints about you could be just around the corner. Backstabbing can cause you to lose the job, because as is the case with most gossip, your complaints could get back to her. Just as important is not backstabbing your employees. Your options are similar. Either try to improve the working relationship (check out tips in chapter 4, page 78) or fire the employee. Talking behind someone's back occurs when someone doesn't want to confront another person. It is a weak and borderline dishonest maneuver that won't win the respect of the people around you.

always tell the truth, even when it hurts

You are in an honorable position as a manager and you need to respect what that role represents to those above and those below. Your boss has entrusted you to be up-front about what is going on with your team, your successes and failures. Don't lie to them about sales you haven't made, projects you haven't finished, employees you haven't yet reviewed. If you are less than honest even once, they will begin to question all of the information you are presenting to them. This also holds true for the team. Be honest with them about how they are doing, share customer feedback, and let them know if the company is on target with goals. Obviously, don't tell them proprietary information, but always tell them the truth. Even if it is negative feedback, there is a professional way to present it to your employees. Telling the truth is harder sometimes than not, so the manager who is striving to be a leader should always be honest.

miss manners: say please and thank you

"There's no excuse for bad manners." How many times have we heard that? It was good advice then and it is good advice now, although some managers may have forgotten. The *Phoenix Business Journal* reported that in a study conducted by etiquette consultants Eticon Inc., 80 percent of the respondents reported an increase of rudeness in business. When they encounter rudeness, 58 percent of the people surveyed said they will take their business elsewhere. "Rude behavior ruins business," said Ann Humphries, Eticon president.

A number of good books have been written on business etiquette that will help you brush up on your skills. We like *The Etiquette Advantage in Business: Personal Skills for Professional Success* by Peggy and Peter Post (third generation descendants of Emily Post), *Power Etiquette: What You Don't Know Can Kill Your Career* by Dana May Casperson, and *Manners That Sell: Adding the Polish that Builds Profits* by Lydia Ramsey.

Here are some tips from Lydia Ramsey on making a good first impression:

- Remember that you are always onstage. At any given moment you may encounter that sought-after client or potential employer. Always be prepared to look and sound your best.
- Focus on the other person. Use the person's name immediately in conversation.
- Smile and make eye contact. You will make other people feel good about themselves and about you.

stealing stinks: keep those hands out of the cookie jar

Of course we're not talking about removing people's property. That is obviously and horribly wrong. What we're talking about are the two common forms of theft in the workplace: stealing ideas and stealing time.

Idea stealers don't last long. Eventually they will be caught. They may get away with it for a while, but those who you are stealing from will catch on fast and soon there will be only silence when you're in the room. Sooner or later, you've got to stand on your own and either do the job or not. Taking other people's ideas—like taking credit for their work—is not for anyone who wants to be a good manager. Working with people on good ideas is a different story.

Sitting at your desk checking personal e-mails, instant messaging friends, planning vacations, or shopping for bargains, if done regularly, is stealing time from your organization. And stealing time means stealing money. The long hours that we all keep now require us to handle some personal business while we are at our workplace. However, as managers, it is important to set an example. Don't abuse the privilege or allow your staff to either. Keep track of how much time everyone is losing to personal business, and if it gets out of control and work begins to suffer, then start banning personal time on the computer.

just say you're sorry

As Hugh Grant proved when he apologized on *The Tonight Show with Jay Leno* for cheating on his girlfriend Elizabeth Hurley with a prostitute, no mistake is big enough that an apology won't cure it. During her insider trading scandal, legal analysts were begging Martha Stewart to apologize. She refused and went to jail.

Not all apologies are created equal, however. In *Psychology Today*, Dr. Aaron Lazare suggests that there is a right and wrong way to offer a sincere apology. If you don't include some crucial elements, your apology is likely to fail.

Here are the components of a good apology:

- Be specific and take responsibility for the impact of your transgression. "I'm sorry for my mistake" is not enough. "I am sorry that I sent an unapproved press release out to the media and jeopardized our client" is better. It acknowledges that you know what you did wrong and why it's important.
- Explain why you messed up and let the injured party know that you learned from your mistake and it won't happen again.
- Make sure you communicate that it wasn't personal, so you can regain trust in the relationship.
- You have to show a little suffering—for your apology to be believed the injured party has to be able to see you sweat a little. It shows that this situation really matters to you.

Finally, nothing undermines a good apology more than repeatedly making the same mistake. We have a staff member who is always late. Almost every day, she comes in with a heartfelt apology and excuse for her tardiness. We've lost interest in both the apologies and the excuses. We simply want her to get to work on time.

good witch or big bitch?

WHY IS SHE SO CRAZY?

Jennifer Mitchell moved to New York from San Francisco to take a job at a marketing company where, unbeknownst to her, there'd been several rounds of layoffs in the year prior to her arrival. She realized pretty quickly that she'd landed in a bitter and deflated environment composed of paranoid employees. Here's her story:

On my first day, my boss "Linda" took me to lunch, and by the time we finished our sandwiches, I knew of the dozens of shortcomings my colleagues allegedly possessed. It was a little unsettling, especially when she used words like "incompetent" and "clueless" about a vice president named "Paul" she'd inherited when the tech department had dissolved. Even stranger, she instructed me to supervise "Paul" despite his seniority to me.

After a few weeks as Linda's Golden Girl, the other shoe dropped. I expected it would, given the way she spoke about my colleagues, but never imagined how bad it would get. Looking back, it seemed to start when my team had to move to the other end of the office. Instead of moving me with them, she put me in an office that was a good thirty-second (brisk) walk from Linda and the rest of the team. Linda was rarely in her office, which I'd soon discovered after making many trips back and forth several times a day. I'd go days at a time without seeing her and it began to impact our relationship. She also frequently withheld critical information about our company and my clients, and didn't invite me to several important meetings, only to then accuse me of negligence and lack of commitment to my work. I explained that, with respect to her busy schedule, I hadn't had access to some important information and meetings, that I'd had no way of knowing about x, y, or z, and would like it if we could set up a weekly one-on-one and/or e-mail update to ensure that we were on the same page. "I'm not your mother, Jennifer, and I can't be expected to hold your hand—you need to be more proactive," was her response.

A few weeks after the move, she began to find fault with virtually everything I did. By the way, an important thing to note is that "Paul," the incompetent, clueless VP, had been moved to an office next door to Linda's. Suddenly they seemed to be very chummy, and my initial paranoia about them conspiring to push me and a couple of other colleagues out was soon confirmed.

I took a late evening call on my cell phone from clients in California who'd just received a final and long-awaited government approval and urgently wanted to meet with me in person to ramp up. They thought that, since I was going to San Francisco (home) for Thanksgiving, it would be ideal to extend the trip by one day so I could go to their offices for a meeting. Well trained by that point, and paranoid that they reached me directly without a hall pass from Linda, I made no commitments other than saying I'd discuss it with Linda and the team and get back to them. I immediately left detailed voice-mails for both Linda and Paul. At 10:00 p.m. that night, Linda called my apartment. Thankfully, my boyfriend was there for this conversation, because I'm not sure anyone would have ever believed it. In a nutshell, she not only accused me of breaking specific and "official" orders about client contact, but she also said the following: "I am stunned and appalled by your behavior today." When I asked her if she'd checked her e-mail and voice-mail to fully understand the nature of the conversation I'd had, she said, "that's irrelevant."

She went on, "Jennifer, I'm no psychologist, but I would honestly suggest you seek some help to figure out what your motives are for your behavior. You seem to be a very troubled young woman." After about ten minutes of other attempts to make me feel awful and reconsider whether the company was a good fit for me, she said, "And in addition, I have documented evidence that you broke into my e-mail account and read and deleted my e-mails on a few occasions."

At the end of this call, she said the most important thing was for me to have a wonderful Thanksgiving with my family. And by the time I arrived in SF the following day, she'd left three messages *on my cell phone, the last one to this effect: "Jennifer, I just wanted to say thanks again for your hard work and efforts with the client yesterday. Please don't worry about scheduling a meeting while you're in the Bay Area. It's your vacation, and I want you to enjoy it. But you did great work, thank you. And we'll see you when you get back to the office."*

Needless to say, I resigned upon my return with as much grace as I could muster, keeping faith in karma whenever I fantasized about submitting a first-person account with real names to a trade magazine. When Linda called a staff meeting to announce my res-ignation, she positioned it as a very disappointing piece of news and said that I was a very talented specialist and would be missed.

Big Bitch. This boss was clearly paranoid, manipulative, unprofes-sional, and untrustworthy. She clearly should not have been put in charge of any*thing*, never mind any*one*. She is the type of back-stabbing, game-playing head case that gives the rest of us women managers a bad name. We can't imagine that her career went far, although sometimes these types of corporate sharks swim right up to the top.

don't be a bully: being the boss doesn't make you queen of the hill

According to the Workplace Bullying and Trauma Institute (yes, it really exists—check it out at www.bullyinginstitute.org), an abusive boss is more likely to be a woman than a man. Woman-to-woman bullying represents 50 percent of all workplace bullying; man-to-woman is 30 percent, man-to-man 12 percent, and woman-to-man bullying is extremely rare—only 8 percent.

Harry Levinson, Ph.D., the dean of organizational psychologists and head of the Levinson Institute in Waltham, Massachusetts, ad-mits that there has been no comprehensive study on "bully bosses";

however, organizational psychologists agree that they exist. After almost forty years in consulting with companies, he has identified the common characteristics of bully bosses. "Bully bosses overcontrol, micromanage, and display contempt for others, usually by repeated verbal abuse and sheer exploitation. They constantly put others down with snide remarks or harsh, repetitive, and unfair criticism. They don't just differ with you, they differ with you contemptuously; they question your adequacy and your commitment. They humiliate you in front of others."

The Workplace Bullying and Trauma Institute has categorized the bullies. Take a look at them and make sure you don't fit the bill. If you do fit any of these bullying types, then you might want to consider taking an anger management course or speaking to human resources about signing you up for a leadership workshop. The bottom line is that you can't lead effectively if you bully your employees.

- "Constant Critics" use put-downs, insults, and name-calling to intimidate. If this is you, then put yourself in your employee's place. Would this motivate you? We didn't think so.
- "Two-headed snakes" pretend to be nice, while all the while they try to sabotage the team. No one likes a backstabber. Your team is counting on you to be up-front with them, good, bad, and ugly.
- "Gatekeepers" are obsessed with control—they allocate time, money, and staffing to ensure their target's failure. Control freaks ultimately want to control subordinates' ability to network in the company or to shine. If this is you, then you most likely have noticed your constant stream of assistants. If they succeed, you succeed.
- "Screaming Mimis" are emotionally out of control and explosive. You need help if this is you. So sign yourself up for an anger management class . . . ASAP.

play fair: cheaters never win and winners
never cheat

We're a nation of cheaters. We cheat on our taxes. We cheat on our spouses. We cheat on our diets. David Callahan, author of *The Cheating Culture: Why More Americans Are Doing Wrong to Get Ahead*, the first exhaustive look at cheating in America, explains on his Web site, www.cheatingculture.com, that more people cheat now because the pressure to succeed is so much higher, starting at an earlier age. Any parent in New York City will tell you that if you don't get your child into the right preschool, then the child will never get into the right college. Callahan also concludes that if you cheat and get away with it at a young age, you're more likely to cheat as an adult and in your workplace.

Companies and managers need to adopt zero-tolerance policies for cheating. In the post–Enron, WorldCom, and Tyco worlds, organizations need to be vigilant about telling the truth and representing their finances accurately to their employees and the public. Fudging budgets, padding expense reports, and fixing time cards are disciplinary offenses that should lead to termination.

girl talk

LINDA GREENLAW, AUTHOR AND CAPTAIN

Linda Greenlaw loves fishing. She is the only woman to ever captain a swordfishing boat, working the waters east of the Grand Banks of Newfoundland. She captained the *Hannah Boden*, the sister boat of the *Andrea Gail*, made famous in the book *The Perfect Storm* by Sebastian Junger. Junger described Greenlaw as "one of the best captains, period, on the entire East Coast." Starting out as a cook and deckhand aboard a swordboat during her summer breaks from Colby College in Maine, Linda had worked her way into the captain's chair by 1986.

She traded in her captain's chair on the swordboat for her own lobsterboat. She works it inshore with her father, lobstering the water surrounding her home on Isle au Haut, a small island off the coast of Maine. She has written four books: *The Hungry Ocean: A Swordboat's Captain Journey*; *The Lobster Chronicles: Life on a Very Small Island*; *All Fishermen Are Liars: True Tales from the Dry Dock Bar*; and her most recent, *Recipes from a Very Small Island*, which she wrote with her mother.

With the exception of her book publicist and her mother, Greenlaw has never worked for, with, or around women. There were no women crews and no woman has ever asked her for a job. Linda's professional experience is wholly unique, yet she shared lessons that will benefit us all.

Why were there no women in your professional life?

Commercial fishing is not an industry on the rise. More people are getting out, not getting in, and I think it is a job that young women today wouldn't even consider. All the people involved with the fishing industry, the ones who buy the fish, sell the fish, sell the bait, and handle the gear are all men. Fishing is my first love. I didn't care that I was surrounded by men, because all I cared about was my own performance.

Can you describe your management philosophy? And how did you develop it?

I never thought about a philosophy per se, but I suppose if I had to come up with one, I would say I treat people the way I want to be treated. I don't enjoy people who are bossy or loud, so I don't act that way.

I started at the bottom—you can't get much lower than a cook on a fishing boat. I was the "green guy" (lowest guy on the boat) when I was nineteen. I worked for some men who were screamers and I've worked for and around men who are gentlemen. It's been a fifty-fifty proposition. I would imagine the boat is like everywhere else. Some people are a lot easier to get along with than others, but if you do the best that you can and treat everyone with respect, you'll have a better chance of succeeding.

We would imagine it was pretty difficult to be taken seriously as a woman fisherman. How did you earn the respect of the others?
I found something I loved to do. I worked very hard at it. I got good at it. Through the years, I worked every job on the boat. When you ask most people their description of a fisherman, they describe a great big, strong man. Most people think fishing requires brute strength. I've found fishing is not about brute strength, but about mental strength and physical endurance. As a 125-pound woman who stands at five-foot-three, I had to find new ways to do things.

I had a captain, Alden Leeman, nicknamed Screamin' Leeman, from whom I learned a lot about fishing and nothing at all about handling people. I worked for Alden first as a cook, then a deckhand, and then a first mate. Becoming a captain in many ways is about staying on a boat long enough to get a chance. When Alden bought a second boat, he needed a captain and gave me a chance.

What qualities did you look for in your crew?
Looking for a job on a fishing boat is called looking for a "site." Guys would come up looking for a site and I would ask questions. "I need someone who can cook." "I need an engineer." "Do you know this type of engine or refrigeration system?"

If there is one thing I know, it is that people lie to get jobs. I've found the guy who says the least about himself usually turns out to be the best. The ones who are really trying to convince you how skilled they are never turn out to be the best workers. The guy who simply says "I'm a hard worker" was always the guy I wanted on my boat.

Also, I didn't want input, I wanted work. I didn't care how they did it on another captain's boat. If they liked that way so much, they could go work for them.

The best guy to have on the boat was a guy capable of doing

my job but who didn't want my job. He wanted to be the best crew member he could.

And how did you find them?

If you're top producer, everybody wants to crew for you. If you're fortunate enough to surround yourself with the best people possible, you will be that much more successful. When I was running the *Hannah* boat, the Cadillac of the fleet, everyone just walked on and jumped into their role. A swordfishing trip lasts thirty days and is run by a five- or six-man crew and everybody works together. There's a butcher, someone to handle the tackle, an engineer, the first mate, and the "green guy" or the cook. Everybody has to pay attention and there can't be one weak link. When there was a new person, he was never in charge of the "mission critical" jobs. For example, he would never be in charge of cleaning fish. If the fish rot during the trip, it's a disaster. Green guys were charged with things that they could take a lot of pride in and that were critical to the success of the trip, but couldn't lose us a lot of money or get anyone killed.

How did people react to a woman captain?

In the beginning it was funny. Some guy would come along the deck and ask me if my husband was aboard. When I told them I didn't have a husband, they would then ask if the captain was aboard. When I replied that I was the captain, you could see the look register on their face. They were thinking, "Oh God, I guess I've blown it." Once I got more established, it was never an issue.

It doesn't sound like you needed to be a bitch to be respected. How did you do it?

I pride myself on not being a bitch. It takes a lot of work to be bitchy. If you're fishing, it's a twenty-four-hour-a-day exhausting job. Being a bitch would make it that much harder. I think I was successful because I worked harder. It's my nature to work hard and gender never entered the picture. I never felt responsible for representing women. I represent only Linda Greenlaw. I just am myself and I don't want to be a role model. I love fishing and want to be good at it. Being a woman is something completely out of my control. It's simply a fact. Being a great fisherman is what I worked hard to do. Now I am putting my energy into doing the best job that I can writing and promoting my books. This may sound silly, but now I am fishing for readers and booksellers. I know if I do a good job for them, then they will do a good job for me and continue to support me and buy and sell more of my books.

a final note

We were recently invited to a fund-raising gala for the Center for the Advancement of Women, where we had the privilege and honor of hearing both Gloria Steinem and Madeleine Albright talk about the importance of helping other women succeed. Madeleine Albright said "there's a special place in hell for women who don't help out other women," which got a big laugh while at the same time inspiring all of us to think about the responsibility we have to our sisters. We know this sounds a little "I am woman hear me roar," but we really want to encourage all of you reading this book to be more mentor than manager. Be aware of your own internalized sexism and commit to not judging your female employees for not being more like the men in the office. Appreciate the diversity. Encourage your female employees to contribute and speak up, support their professional growth and development right along with your male reports. You have the opportunity to be the agent of change in your employees' life, to be their "Good Witch" story, and we hope that you make the commitment to master this challenging and often wonderful role of being someone's boss.

resources

BOOKS

Leadership/Management

Autry, James A. *The Servant Leader: How to Build A Creative Team, Develop Great Morale, and Improve Bottom-Line Performance*. New York: Three Rivers Press, 2001.

Belbin, Meredith. *Management Teams: Why They Succeed or Fail*. New York: Butterworth-Heinemann, 2003.

Blanchard, Ken, and Spencer Johnson. *One Minute Manager*. New York: William Morrow, 1983.

Blanchard, Ken, and Patricia Zigarmi. *Leadership and the One Minute Manager*. New York: William Morrow, 1999.

Glaser, Judith. *Creating We: Change I-Thinking to WE-Thinking and Build a Healthy, Thriving Organization*. Avon, Mass.: Platinum Press, 2005.

McBee, Shar. *To Lead Is to Serve*. Loma Linda, Cal.: SMB Publishing, 2002.

Templar, Richard. *Rules of Management*. Englewood Cliffs, N.J.: Prentice Hall, 2005.

Women/Business

Evans, Gail. *Play Like a Man, Win Like a Woman: What Men Know About Success that Women Need to Learn.* New York: Broadway Books, 2000.

———. *She Wins, You Win: The Most Important Strategies for Making Women More Powerful.* New York: Gotham, 2004.

Weisberger, Lauren. *The Devil Wears Prada.* New York: Doubleday, 1977.

Inspirational Memoirs

Greenlaw, Linda. *All Fishermen Are Liars.* New York: Hyperion, 2004.

———. *The Hungry Ocean: A Swordboat Captain's Journey.* New York: Hyperion, 1999.

———. *The Lobster Chronicles: Life on a Very Small Island.* New York: Hyperion, 2003.

———. *Recipes from a Very Small Island.* New York: Hyperion, 2005.

Junger, Sebastian. *The Perfect Storm: A True Story of Men Against the Sea.* New York: Harper Torch, 1998.

A Cookbook from Our Name It/Claim It Oprah Girl

Martinez, Daisy. *Daisy Cooks!* New York: Hyperion, 2005.

Etiquette

Callahan, David. *The Cheating Culture: Why More Americans Are Doing Wrong to Get Ahead.* New York: Harcourt, 2004.

Casperson, Dana May. *Power Etiquette: What You Don't Know Can Kill Your Career.* New York: American Management Association, 1999.

Post, Peter, and Peggy Post. *The Etiquette Advantage in Business: Personal Skills for Professional Success.* New York: HarperCollins, 1999.

Ramsey, Lydia. *Manners That Sell: Adding the Polish That Builds Profits.* Boston: Longfellow Press, 2000.

Entrepreneurship

Friedman, Caitlin, and Kimberly Yorio. *The Girl's Guide to Starting Your Own Business.* New York: HarperCollins, 2004.

ARTICLES

Bragg, Terry. "Nine Strategies for Successfully Playing Office Politics." *Occupational Hazards*. 2004. Feb 2004:49

WEB SITES

General Research
www.about.com
www.ivillage.com

Etiquette
www.cheatingculture.com

Venting Blogs
www.iworkwithfools.com
www.fthisjob.com
www.oddtodd.com
www.revengelady.com

Women Leaders
www.guide2womenleaders.com
www.leadingfromthefront.com

Hiring and Firing
www.dol.gov
www.office-politics.com
www.payscale.com
www.quintcareers.com/web_master.html
www.ustechnicaljobs.com
www.monster.com
www.careerbuilder.com
www.theladders.com

Entrepreneurship

www.onlinewbc.gov

Management Training

Center for Creative Leadership

www.ccl.org

www.haygroup.com

index

A

A&E Television, 153
alcohol and drinking, 92
Andrews, Leah, 151
Andrus, Mark, 22
apologies, 201–2
appreciation/gratitude, xi, 24, 31, 88,
    111–13, 191
Arsht, Adrienne, 58

B

Barns, Sarah, 145
Baron, Anat, 52, 95
Baron, Ayelet, 64
Bates, Diane, 132–34
Belbin, Meredith, 36
birthdays, 111–12
Blackwell, Deborah, 75–77
Blake, Lisa, 86–88
Blake, Tammy, 59
blame, accepting, 5, 35, 195–96, 197
Blanchard, Ken, 29–30
blogs, workplace, 187–90

Blue Sky Communications, 132
Bodge, Trae, 87
boundaries, employee, 71, 72, 131–32
Bragg, Terry, 177
Brierty, Linda, 18–20
budget and spending, 11
bullying, 205–6
Burke, Claire, 157
business manners and etiquette, 179,
    200
business plan, 9

C

Callahan, David, 207
career development, 74, 83, 104–6,
    133
Catwoman (movie), 7
Center for the Advancement of
    Women, 213
Center for Women's Business
    Research, 175–76
cheating, 207
Cheating Culture, The (Callahan), 207

Circuit Productions, Inc., 119
Colabella, Chris, 111, 139–40
communication, 34–36, 98–100, 101–2
    apologies, 201–2
    chitchat, 131–32
    corporate culture and, 166–68
    day-to-day performance, 137–38
    goals of company, conveying, 157
    ideas, employee, 198
    information sharing, 195
    Johari Window, 168–71
    listening attentively, 132
    See also evaluations and reviews
compensation and salary, 109–11, 157
Condé Nast magazines, 164–65
confidence boosters, 19–20
confidentiality, 183
conflict resolution, 89, 130–31
Construction Information Systems, 139
corporate culture, 155–74
    assessing, questions to ask, 156
    clashes, geography and, 166–68
    dress codes, 155, 160–64
    evaluating, *Fortune* survey, 157–58
    mission statement and values, 158–59
Costello, Amy, 196–97
Craig, David, 153–54
Creating We (Glaser), 101, 160–61
credit for ideas/work products, 7, 93, 133–34, 195, 201
Curry, Amy, 61–62
Cutler, Jessica, 189

D

Dale, Krista, 164–65
Daphne Foundation, 69, 144
dating, workplace, 183–85, 193
deadlines, 15, 35, 70
Deane, Julie, 173–74

delegating work, 9–10, 70, 73, 86, 87–88, 92–93, 117–23
    avoiding personal requests, 89, 133
    dumping, 119–20
    mentor for, example, 128–30
    See also micromanaging
Deussen, Christine, 68–69
Deussen Global Communications, 68, 95
Disclosure (movie), 7
Disney, Abigail, 69, 144
Donna Karan International, 160–61
dress codes, 155, 160–64
Duffy, Laurice, 31

E

Edelman and Intelliseek, 189
e-mail, 91
emotions in the workplace or public, 9, 17, 18–19, 23, 38, 94, 96, 97
employee types, 30–32
entrepreneurs, 16, 52
    creating a culture, 165, 171–74
    hiring decisions for, 54
evaluations and reviews, 9, 136–45
    Colabella's program for, 140
    day-to-day monitoring, 137–38
    five common mistakes, 142–44
    importance of, 138–39
    mistakes of employee, 151, 196
    sample review, "BEST" system, 140–42
    warnings and performance, 144–45
Eticon Inc., 200
Evans, Gail, 176

F

Fair Labor Standards Act (FLSA), 109
fear
    delegating and, 19, 118–19

leading with, 8, 122

tips before facing your staff, 118–19

feedback and criticism, 19, 30–31, 35, 68, 71, 87, 96, 199

day-to-day monitoring and, 137–38

Johari Window use of, 170

Ferraro, Geraldine, 17

film, depiction of women bosses, 6–8

firing, xi, 6, 9, 23, 88–89, 144–50

blogging and, 189–90

exit interview, 149–50

legal liability and, 139, 147–50

severance package, 148

first impressions, 200

Fortune, company evaluation, 157–58

Fresh Partners, 159

friendship and/or workplace socializing, 4, 7, 63, 69–70, 74, 82–83, 90, 96, 183–85, 186, 193

G

Gawker.com, 187–88

gender differences

in leadership, 44–45, 47, 74, 96, 153–54, 175–77

discrimination and, 18–19, 33, 83

managing men vs. women, 73–74, 77

women supporting women, 97, 213

Glamour magazine, 175

Glaser, Judith, 101–3, 160–61

goal-setting, 14–15, 107–9, 127–28

Goldbetter, Susan, 119

gossip, workplace, 181–83

Graham, Tessa Jane, 159–60

Grant, Hugh, 201

Greenlaw, Linda, 207–11

Grettacole salons, 157, 171–74

guiding/directing employees, 10–11, 35

H

Hansen, Randall, 156

hiring, 9, 23–24, 51–56, 66, 188, 209–10

assistant position, 59–60

avoiding head games/power trips, 57

entrepreneurs, tips for, 54

interviewing, 55–56

legalities, 54–55

Horowitz, Phil, 183

Humphries, Ann, 200

Hunter Public Relations, 157

Hutchenson, Kathleen, 69–70

I

information sharing, 160, 195

Ingham, Harry, 168, 170

InnVest REIT, 120

insecurity about position, 19, 79–80

InStyle, 164

Internet sites

advancingwomen.com, 10

blogs, workplace, 187–90

bullyinginstitute.org, 205

cheatingculture.com, 207

cisleads.com, 139

complaints about job, various sites, 99

Department of Labor, 109

fresh-partners.com, 159

grettacole.com, 171

guide2womenleaders.com, 25

job opportunities-job search sites, 52

lawyers.com, 175

leadingfromthefront.com, 43

legalities of hiring and firing, 55

mission statements, 158

office-politics.com, 191

ustechnicaljobs.com, 40, 42

Women's Business Center, 162

J

Jacobs, Dorri, 88–89, 130
James, Franke, 191–93
jealousy, 95, 96
job descriptions, 89–90
Johari Window, 168–71
Jones, Aleta, 106–7
Jordan, Louise, 95–97
Junger, Sebastian, 207

K

Kill Bill (movie), 6–7
Kleiman, Janie, 145
Kramer, Beth, 63–64
Kramer, Ilene, 196
Kyle, Jennifer, 137

L

LaBelle, Patti, 60
late-night etiquette, 113
Lawson, Tamara, 120
Laybourne, Gerry, 144
Lazare, Aaron, 202
LDK Cleaning Service, 31
leadership. *See* management
*Leadership and the One Minute
    Manager* (Blanchard), 29–30
Lead Star company, 43, 47
Leeman, Alden, 209
Levinson, Harry, 205–6
Luft, Joe, 168, 170
Lynch, Courtney, 43–47
Lynn, Donna, 198

M

Madison, Stacy, 22–24
Malkin, Amie, 42, 167–68
Malkin, Laurie, 54–55, 147–50
management, 1–2, 14, 16, 17, 19, 23
    behaviors that fail/succeed, 24,
        102–3
    benefits/losses of joining, 2–6,
        26

crazy or unreasonable bosses,
        12–13, 82, 106–7, 164–65,
        180–81, 203–5, 206
    gender differences, leadership,
        44–45, 47, 96, 153–54, 175–77
    gender differences, managing
        men vs. women, 73–74
    gender discrimination, 18–19, 33,
        83
    kindergarten lessons for, 196–97
    leadership strengths and
        weaknesses, 34–36, 45–46, 47,
        76, 79–80
    personality traits and testing for,
        39–43
    role of, fifteen duties, 14–18
    signs, being taken advantage of,
        70–73
    ten ways to alienate staff, 78–97
    tips, good/effective managing,
        134–35
    transparency, 160
management styles, 76
    bullying, 205–6
    firm but fair, 27–29
    "give" side, 114–16
    ineffective or destructive, 78–97
    leading by example, 81, 208–9
    situational leadership, 29–32
Management Teams (Belbin), 36
Martinez, Daisy, 107–8
McBee, Shar, 113–16
Mediabistro.com, 187
meetings, 72–73, 103–4, 123–26,
        170
    agenda, 123–24
    lateness to, dealing with, 123
    pre-meeting, senior staff, 124
mentor, 77
    for employees, 3, 144
    system, for training, 58–59
    for yourself, 18, 128–30
micromanagement, 84–86, 138

quiz: are you too controlling?,
    85–86
Miller, Frances, 147
Mitchell, Jennifer, 203–5
Monahan, Gretchen, 157, 171–74
Morgan, Angela, 43–47
motivating (inspiring) employees,
    10–11, 12–13, 24, 76, 113
Myers-Briggs Type Indicator, 40

N

Nasatir, Marcia, 154
networking, 17, 112
"Nine Strategies for Successfully
    Playing Office Politics" (Bragg),
    178–79
Nolan, Dianne, 65–67
Northwestern University Women's
    Lacrosse Team, 163
Norton, Sarilee, 38, 111, 112, 170–71

O

office politics, 175–93
    gossip, workplace, 181–83
    managing your manager, 11,
        185–85
    "must never dos," 192–93
    nine strategies for, 178–79
    whistle-blowing, 192
    workplace dating, 183–85, 193
Office-Politics® game, 191
101 Dalmations (movie), 8
open-door policy, 7, 98
organizational chart, 49
Oxygen Media, 144

P

Peacemakers Training, 177
Perfect Storm, The (Junger), 207
Perkins, Paige, 128–30
personality traits and testing for,
    39–43
    free online test, 40

personal problems, 4–5, 69, 74
Pine, Mindy, 82–83
Play Like a Man, Win Like a Woman
    (Evans), 176
positive outlook, 21–22, 162, 197
praise or positive reinforcement, 96,
    112, 122, 179
preparation, 92
proactive approach, 15
productivity, xi
    careless and/or casual job, 71–72
    lack of, dealing with, 70
    taking on employee's work, 73
    warning about sub-standard,
        144–45
    See also evaluations and reviews
progress reports, 10, 30, 32, 86,
    140
promotions and raises, xi, 9, 136

Q

Quintessential Careers, 156
quiz: are you too controlling?, 85–86

R

Raising Helen (movie), 7
Ramsey, Lydia, 200
relationships in the workplace, 6,
    173–74
    advocate role, 12, 75
    consistency in, 7, 9, 151, 198–99
    dating, workplace, 183–85, 193
    helping your boss succeed, 178–79
    managing your manager, 185–86
    professional distance from
        employees, 4, 63, 69–70, 77,
        82–83, 90, 96, 139
    selling your accomplishments,
        16–17
    standing up for yourself, 17
resignation of employee, 51, 151–52
role model
    acting as, 35, 91–92

example, 61–62
finding, 38–39
Rose, Sharon, 139
Rosen, Ilene, 131
Rosenzweig, Ilene, 160
Rowley, Cynthia, 160

S

Sartain, Libby, 32–33, 99, 104–5
Schulte Roth & Zabel LLP, 54, 147
self-care, 16, 22
sexual harassment, 7, 183–85
She Wins, You Win (Evans), 176
situational leadership, 29–32
SMB Publishing, Inc., 113
SOAPnet, 75
Spiers, Elizabeth, 187–88
Stacy's Pita Chip Company, 22
Stephens, Helen, 79, 83, 89

T

teams, 9, 16, 36, 48–77, 80, 112, 113,
    121, 178, 179
evaluating, 36, 49–51
goal-setting, 107–9
inheriting members, 62–64
key things to provide, 68–69
leadership, 63, 81
management that succeeds, 103
organizational chart for, 49–50
roles in, 36–37
troubleshooting advice, 65–67
work habits to model, 35, 91–92
Teuwen, Stephanie, 53, 55–56
Teuwen One Image, 53
Three Custom Color Specialists, 87
time
lateness, dealing with, 123, 202

management of, 20–21, 115–16
promptness, 92, 197
stealing, 71, 201
See also deadlines
to-do list, 14, 30, 87, 91, 119
Tolleson, Juli, 84–85, 145
TotalBank, Miami, 58
training, xi, 27–29, 30, 58–59, 113
classes, as rewards, 111
management, 3–4, 80
sample first day plan, 59
Tru Tech Business, Temple Inland,
    111
truthfulness, 199
Truth or Dare (movie), 7
trying to be liked, 4, 139
20th Century Fox Television, 145

U

University of New South Wales, 159
US Concepts, 84, 145

W

Walt Disney Company, 155
Wegman's supermarkets, 157
Women's Business Center, 162
word, keeping, 15
work environment, 7
work habits, 91–92
Working Girl (movie), 7
Workplace Bullying and Trauma
    Institute, 205–6

Y

Yahoo! Inc., 32, 99, 158
YC Media, 37, 140–42, 155, 158